French Warship Crews 1789–1805

1789–1805

From the French Revolution to Trafalgar

Terry Crowdy • Illustrated by Steve Noon

First published in Great Britain in 2005 by Osprey Publishing
Midland House, West Way, Botley, Oxford OX2 0PH, UK
443 Park Avenue South, New York, NY 10016, USA
E-mail: info@ospreypublishing.com

ISBN 1 84176 745 X

A CIP catalogue record for this book is available from the British Library

Editor: Katherine Venn
Design: Edward Moore, Osprey Publishing
Index by Alison Worthington
Originated by Grasmere Digital Imaging, Leeds, UK
Printed in China through World Print Ltd.

05 06 07 08 09   10 9 8 7 6 5 4 3 2 1

FOR A CATALOGUE OF ALL BOOKS PUBLISHED BY OSPREY MILITARY AND AVIATION PLEASE CONTACT:

NORTH AMERICA
Osprey Direct, 2427 Bond Street, University Park, IL 60466, USA
E-mail: info@ospreydirectusa.com

ALL OTHER REGIONS
Osprey Direct UK, P.O. Box 140, Wellingborough,
Northants, NN8 2FA, UK
E-mail: info@ospreydirect.co.uk

Buy online at **www.ospreypublishing.com**

Artist's note

Readers may care to note that the original paintings from which the colour plates in this book were prepared are available for private sale. All reproduction copyright whatsoever is retained by the Publishers. All enquiries should be addressed to:

Steve Noon
50 Colchester Avenue
Penylan
Cardiff
CF23 9BP
UK

The Publishers regret that they can enter into no correspondence upon this matter.

Editor's note

We would like to acknowledge the use made of Général Morand's *Lettres sur l'expédition d'Egypte / Carnets de route de chef de brigade à Assouan 1798–1799*, published in 1998 by LA VOUIVRE in Warrior 77, *French Soldier in Egypt 1798–1801: The Army of the Orient*, Osprey Publishing, Oxford (2003). We are grateful to the family and publisher for letting us use a wide variety of material from this publication.

Author's acknowledgements

Along with the staff of the British Library, I would like to express gratitude to my father, Ron Crowdy, along with Martin Lancaster, David Hollins, Ashley Kane, Alfred Umhey, Yves Martin, Tony 'Louis' Lofts, Christa Hook, Hans-Karl Weiss, Sujatha Iyer, Gerd Hoad, Stéphanie Sauzeau, Steve Vickers and everyone who has offered encouragement, particularly Mr Richard Walduck, OBE, JP, DL.

All illustrations provided courtesy of the Umhey Collection.

CONTENTS

FRENCH WARSHIP CREWS 1789–1805 FROM THE FRENCH REVOLUTION TO TRAFALGAR

INTRODUCTION

It is commonly believed that the French Revolution was a disaster that wrecked a fine navy. Although the *Marine Royale* had enjoyed recent successes in the American Revolution, it already suffered from deep-rooted problems. France was reputed to have the best designed ships in the world, but to build them it was heavily reliant on imported raw materials, including timber from the Baltic and Italy. The living conditions on the king's ships were notoriously dire and the sailors were often left unpaid or cheated out of pensions. Draconian punishments capped the misery of those in service and encouraged sailors to flee inland to avoid the compulsory *inscription maritime*.

There were even problems inside the largely aristocratic officer corps with friction between port officials (the so-called 'officers of the quill') and the seafaring, military officers (or 'officers of the épée'), with outright snobbery shown by all towards non-noble officers drawn from the merchant fleet. Maintaining a fleet was a huge financial burden on the country and so, as France drew towards bankruptcy at the end of the 1780s, the navy's expansionist plans were crippled. The failure to pay dockworkers in Toulon led to riots early in 1789, several months before the storming of the Bastille in Paris on 14 July.

Following the Bastille, riots increased in Toulon. In 1790 the Atlantic fleet mutinied over the introduction of a supposedly fairer penal code. Impotent in the face of growing insubordination and increasingly fearful of their personal safety, the aristocrat-dominated officer corps was decimated by a flood of emigrations. Worse was to follow. With the king guillotined in 1793, the port of Toulon rejected republicanism and declared in favour of the king's imprisoned son, Louis XVII. The town authorities opened the port to the British and the Mediterranean fleet was all but lost. Simultaneously, civil war flared up in the conservative west, leaving France's two principal maritime recruitment areas in

Brest Harbour in 1794 at the time of Jean-Bon Saint-André's mission to restore order and discipline in the navy.

open revolt against the government. Threatened by spreading civil war and foreign invasion, the government struck back, declaring Terror as the order of the day, sending thousands of real and suspected enemies to the guillotine.

Anticipating the outbreak of famine, in December 1793 the French government sent five million pounds of gold to the United States to buy grain and flour. To protect the returning convoy from the British Channel Fleet, the government minister, Jean-Bon Saint-André, oversaw the fitting out of a fleet that put to sea from Brest under the command of Villaret-Joyeuse. At the Battle of 1st June 1794 ('Glorious First of June' for Britain) the French went head-to-head with a British fleet under Lord Howe. Seven French ships were lost, but enough British ships were badly damaged for Howe to call off the pursuit of the convoy, allowing it to reach France safely. Although the battle revealed the inexperience of French crews, their enthusiasm and resolution to give battle received considerable praise from Howe.

During the period of the Directorate (1795–1799), the navy was used in a support role to transport army expeditions to Ireland, Wales and, most famously, Egypt in 1798. Having eluded detection while crossing the Mediterranean and having landed the bulk of the army and its equipment, the expedition's fleet suffered a crushing blow at the hands of Nelson in Aboukir Bay. However, just five years later the French Navy had sufficiently recovered for Britain to fear a cross-Channel invasion. In 1805 the navy was heavily defeated at Trafalgar – but the performance of ships like Captain Lucas' *Redoutable* meant that British victory only came at the loss of their greatest naval leader, Nelson, who was shot during the action.

Because of this mixed record and being eclipsed by the successes of Napoleon's armies on land, comparatively little therefore has been written on the French Navy of the era. Even less has been said of the crews, their occupations, routines and the living conditions they endured at sea. Through contemporary legislation, surviving reports and in particular a number of revealing memoirs, we are now able to take a glimpse back into the world of sailors and soldiers at sea during the First French Republic and early Empire.

Miniature portrait of Villaret-Joyeuse (1747–1812). A *capitaine de vaisseau* **in 1789, he did not emigrate and was promoted to** *contre-amiral* **(rear admiral) on 16 November 1793, becoming commander-in-chief of the Brest Fleet. His moment of destiny came in 1794 during the 'Prairial Campaign', which culminated in the Battle of 1st June ('13 Prairial' to the French) and the safe arrival of a grain convoy from America.**

CHRONOLOGY 1789–1805

1789
24 March: Dockworkers in Toulon protest over unpaid wages;
14 July: Storming of Bastille heralds beginning of French Revolution;
1 December: Rioting in Toulon.
1790
21 August: New penal code provokes Brest mutiny.
1792
20 April: France declares war on Austria and Prussia;
10 August: Tuilleries royal palace stormed, king arrested;
23 August: Brest fleet swears new civic oath;
2–3 September: Mediterranean fleet swears new oath in Toulon;
22 September: Republic proclaimed.

1793

21 January: Louis XVI executed;

1 February: France declares war on Britain;

23 August: Toulon invites an alliance with the British;

5 September: Beginning of The Terror;

13 September: Mutiny breaks out in the Brest fleet anchored in Quiberon Bay;

7 October: Saint-André arrives at Brest to restore discipline and reinvigorate the navy;

10 November: New penal code introduced;

1 December: Toulon recaptured, but most of Mediterranean fleet lost.

1794

10 April: Convoy of 127 merchantmen leaves USA bound for France;

16 May: Saint-André and *Vice-amiral* Villaret-Joyeuse sail from Brest to protect convoy from British Channel fleet;

1 June: Battle of 1st June – tactical French defeat with the loss of seven ships, but grain convoy reaches port safely;

27 July: End of The Terror as government overthrown.

1796

21–27 December: French expedition unable to land at Bantry Bay, Ireland.

1797

21 July: French troops landed near Fishguard, Wales.

1798

19 May: Fleet departs Toulon carrying Napoleon's army to Egypt;

10 June: Napoleon successfully invades Malta;

19 June: Napoleon leaves Malta;

30 June: French begin landing troops near Alexandria;

7 July: French fleet moves from Alexandria to Aboukir Bay;

24 July: Napoleon enters Cairo;

1–2 August: Battle of the Nile. French fleet destroyed at anchor in Aboukir Bay;

22 August: French troops landed at Killala Bay, Ireland.

1799

24 August: Napoleon quits Egypt;

17 December: Napoleon becomes First Consul of the Republic.

1800

5 September: French garrison at Malta surrenders to the British.

1801

6 July: Engagement with British at Algeciras;

2 September: French in Egypt capitulate.

La Montagne by Loutherbourg, 1794. 'One noticed then that every ship had her different character, just like men,' remembered Moreau de Jonnes. 'Some always lagged, even under a full spread of canvas, whilst others invariably led even under little sail, and we could estimate what each might be expected to do in action.'

Napoleon and his staff at Boulogne during the build-up to the planned invasion of England. Napoleon planned to land 160,000 men in Britain, a figure dwarfing the 30,000 he took to Egypt.

1802
27 March: Treaty of Amiens – peace with Britain;
1803
16 May: Britain declares war on France;
9 October: Franco-Spanish alliance concluded.
1804
18 May: Napoleon Bonaparte proclaimed Emperor of French Republic;
25 May: First plans to invade England;
19 July: Napoleon inspects the invasion camp at Boulogne;
14 December: Spain declares war on Britain.
1805
8 January: Treaty of naval co-operation with Spain;
29 March: Toulon fleet escapes blockade and heads for Atlantic;
22 July: Action as British sight French fleet;
20 August: French and Spanish fleets rendezvous at Cadiz;
27 August: Invasion army quits the Channel coast and heads for Germany;
19 October: Franco-Spanish fleet leaves Cadiz bound for Mediterranean;
21 October: Battle of Trafalgar – 'combined fleet' defeated at the loss of 18 ships.

MARITIME FRANCE

It is estimated that in 1789 there were about 60,000 sailors in France working on 1,800 miles of coastline and inland waterways. Geography compelled France to divide its navy into two different theatres of operation – one on the Mediterranean to the south and the other on the north and west Atlantic coastline – making it difficult for naval forces to concentrate in wartime.

Maritime Agent Port Commander, engraving by Labrousse. Prior to the revolution such *officiers de la plume* were the object of great scorn from military officers.

The coastal provinces and islands were divided into six maritime departments each administered by a chief port. Three of these ports (Toulon, Rochefort and Brest) were home to the great naval arsenals, where *vaisseaux* (ships of the line) could be built and where materials, munitions and supplies were stored. A fourth naval arsenal was constructed at the Atlantic port of Lorient in 1770 after the closure of the French *Compagnie des Indes* (East India Company) the year before. Lacking a major Channel port, work had begun on an artificial harbour at Cherbourg in 1783, which was not fully inaugurated until 1813.

With the furnaces of industrial revolution only recently kindled across the Channel and the concept of mass assembly still a century away, shipbuilding was extraordinarily labour intensive and expensive. Each arsenal, therefore, was a veritable anthill of naval officials and tradesmen, including shipwrights, drillers, pulley-makers, caulkers, sail-makers, blacksmiths, rope-makers, coopers, pit sawyers, convict-labourers, sculptors, painters, soldiers and fire-fighters (in case the vast stocks of timber caught fire).

The hustle and bustle of a port preparing a fleet for sail is well recorded by Moreau de Jonnes, describing Brest in 1794:

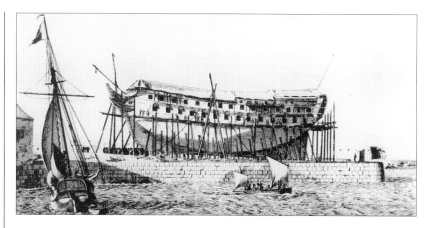

A *vaisseau de 74* under construction. The full scale of the vessel is realized by comparing the size of the workers on the surrounding scaffolding.

From the morning gun, the port teemed with workers loading the ships. Here a mast was being fitted to a ship; there provisions were being transported; launches were embarking troops, further on they were loading the heavy calibre guns, elsewhere barrels of gunpowder. Barges were loaded with cannonballs; boxes of biscuit, sails and cables were brought out of the magazines; convicts heaved at a capstan raising a top mast, top-men put up a yardarm, the gunners practised firing the cannons and the battleships were being towed towards the chain which closed the entrance to the port.

At the outbreak of war with Britain in 1793, the French Navy was estimated to consist of 82 battleships, with frigates and smaller vessels bringing the total to 250 ships. French warships were built to standard designs and were universally considered excellent, although all too often they were left to rot when not commissioned on active service. The top-ranked ships were the *vaisseaux*, which were classed by the number of guns they carried. The largest were the 118-gun *vaisseaux*, followed by the 80- and 74-gun *vaisseaux*, which were more predominant. Conversely, frigates were classed by the calibre of guns they carried, not the quantity. A *frégate de 18* carried 28 18-pounders, while a *frégate de 12* carried 26 12-pounders.

The heaviest-calibre guns were the 36-pounders, which meant they fired a 36lb solid iron ball as their principal projectile. As Table V demonstrates, 36 French pounds was in fact the equivalent of 39 British pounds, making these guns considerably heavier than the 32-pounders commonly used by the Royal Navy. The other gun decks would be armed with 24- and 18-pounders, with 12-pounders on the *galliards* – the quarterdeck and forecastle. Following the British lead, the French had begun to arm their battleships with *carronades*, which they mounted on

I. DISTRIBUTION OF SHIPS' ARMAMENT				
Ship Type	1st deck	2nd deck	3rd deck	*Gaillards*
Vaisseau de 118	32x36pndrs	34x24pndrs	34x12pndrs	20x8pndrs
Vaisseau de 80	30x36pndrs	34x32pndrs	-	16x12pndrs
Vaisseau de 74	28x36pndrs	30x18pndrs	-	16x8pndrs
Frégate de 18	28x18pndrs	-	-	10x8pndrs
Frégate de 12	26x12pndrs	-	-	6x6pndrs

This table does not include the four to six 36-pounder *carronades* mounted on the *galliards* (quarterdeck and forecastle).

the poop deck and forecastle. These weapons were short in range but devastating in effect, firing heavy bursts of canister to sweep personnel from enemy decks and rigging.

The *inscription maritime*

From 1668 all Frenchmen aged 18 and upward exercising one of the maritime professions for over a year were registered on the *rôle des gens de mer* (lit. list of the men of the sea), which made them liable for temporary, yet compulsory, service in the navy when called upon. The list included all the crews and officers of commercial boats engaged in navigation, fishing or on revenue vessels, barges, ferries, launches and other boats on the sea or inland waters.

On qualifying for this *inscription maritime*, which was normally after reaching their eighteenth birthday and having spent a year at sea, the young men were to present themselves with their father or two of their closest relatives at the *bureau d'inscription* where their obligations and rights under the law were explained to them. If they failed to register, went into hiding, or if they joined the land army instead, they would be considered as deserters and their parents would be held responsible.

Under the command of a *commissaire des classes*, each of the maritime departments was divided into *quarts* composed of *syndicats*, each subdivided into *communes*. In each *syndicat* a commissioner would distribute the sailors into four *classes*. The first comprised bachelors; the second, widowers without children; the third, married men without children; the fourth, fathers of families. As and when required, the syndicates were told how many men were needed for naval service. Sailors who volunteered would receive preferential treatment, but in case of a shortfall of volunteers there would be a levy by class. The bachelors would be called up first and exhausted before the second class was called up, and so on through each of the remaining classes. Once called up the men had eight days to arrive in port or be posted as deserters and made subject to the Penal Code. Any captains of commerce who concealed a man that had been called up for service would be stripped of rank and embarked on a warship at the lowest rank.

There were some exemptions, including invalids, men over 50 and men with two sons included in the *inscription*, or who had been killed in action or were recovering from injuries sustained in service. However, even those exempted might still be called on to serve on the harbour guard boats, freeing up active sailors for service on the warships.

In return for this compulsory service, under the *ancien regime* sailors received some significant benefits, including fishing rights, exemption from feudal tithes, free education for their children and a fund for pensioners and the needy. After the Revolution these benefits came to include a state pension, which was pay or half pay according to their rank, age, injury or infirmity, and based on their length of service in both the navy and on commercial shipping. Each year on naval service

Maritime France in 1789. Beginning from the Channel coast, the provinces affected by the *inscription maritime* included Picardy, Flanders, Normandy, Brittany, Poitou, Guienne, the islands of Rhé and Oleron, Languedoc and Provence. These were divided into six *départements* each administered by one of the following ports: Toulon, Bordeaux, Rochefort, Brest, Le Havre and Dunkirk.

Leisure time in the harbour – a watercolour by Ledoux. The *inscription maritime* theoretically put every sailor in France at the navy's disposal and forbade sailors from joining the army on land.

in wartime counted as two years, while a year in peacetime counted as 18 months. Service on merchantmen counted as six months per year in peacetime and a year in wartime. Corsair service (see below) was also recognized, a year's active service counting for 18 months.

The widows and children of sailors had the right to state aid and pensions as accorded to soldiers in the land armies. Artificers were taxed a quarter of their daily pay which was paid directly to their wives in their place of residence. Independent of this, artificers also had to pay a monthly allowance to each of their children over the age of ten, the quantity of which was determined on a case-by-case basis. The children of men on the *inscription maritime* would also get first preference in being admitted as *mousses* (ship's boys), another important concession to those with families.

Although the *inscription maritime* theoretically put every sailor in France at the navy's disposal, there had never been enough men to crew the ships properly. The harsh discipline, the high mortality rates (as much through sickness as combat) and the government's frequent inability to pay the sailors led to a high desertion rate. The Revolution and subsequent outbreak of European war made it even harder to provide crews for the ships.

The most pressing circumstances that contributed to the collapse of the recruiting system in the 1790s are given in a naval commission report made by Boulay-Paty to the government on 14 March 1799:

> The *inscription maritime*, the best of institutions established by the old ordinances under the name of *classes de la marine*, finds itself at this moment entirely disorganized. The war in the Vendée, in particular the disorders around the district of Nantes, the brigandage and *chouannerie* [anti-government rebellion], which, by the lure of pillage, has attracted navy deserters from the ports of Brest and Lorient; the dismissal of all the sailors in Brest for four months, the licentiousness and revolutionary troubles in the south, the capture of Toulon, the death and emigration of part of this port's sailors; the reverse of Aboukir; the large number of sailors escaping the inscription because of badly interpreted laws;

the protection accorded to a number of individuals exempted from service; the majority of novices who, to avoid embarkation have since 1793 joined the armies on land, despite the contrary dispositions of the law in this regard … the uselessness of payments since the discredit of paper-money and the default of payments since its replacement by cash; the inaccuracy in the pay of pensions and family deductions …

So the list went on. A key problem alluded to elsewhere in this report was that the government could not secure the exchange of the 'elite sailors prisoner in England'. In previous wars that century there had been frequent prisoner exchanges between France and Britain. However, the bitterness of the struggle against Revolutionary France meant that there was very little contact between the warring states. On the rare occasions that an exchange was arranged, France often had too few British prisoners to offer in exchange for the return of their countrymen.

To these burdens should also be added the popularity of service onboard *corsairs* – the French privateers operating out of the Channel ports like Dunkirk, Boulogne and Saint-Malo in Brittany. In contrast to the navy, the corsairs were reaping millions in prize money from attacking rich British merchantmen. Sailors would sign up for a ship fitted out by an *armateur* (the ship owner) for a fixed percentage of the prize money. It is easy to understand how some preferred this freewheeling and profitable vocation rather than submit to naval service. Napoleon later felt forced to impose a limit: only an eighth of the corsair crews could be drawn from men on the *inscription*.

THE MEN OF THE SEA

Captain and sailor from Marseille – engraving by Labrousse. Notice the dress of the republican-era captain, with striped trousers and sash. The object in his right hand is a speaking trumpet used to project the officer's voice.

French warships were commanded by an *état-major* (staff) comprising the officers (a *capitaine de vaisseau*, a *capitaine de frégate*, *lieutenants de vaisseau* and *ensignes de vaisseau*), *aspirants* (equivalent to midshipmen), the chief medical officer and a purser. The crew was made up of *officier-mariners* (equivalent to British petty officers), artisans, gunners, soldiers, matelots, novices, boys and a number of supernumeraries including cooks and medical orderlies. Before introducing each group in turn, there is an important observation to be made on French crews. As a rule of thumb, there were ten crewmen for every gun on the ship, which meant that, on paper at least, French crews were larger than their British or Dutch counterparts. In 1798 Baron Lescallier commented that these larger crews were at a disadvantage because they needed more supplies, suffered more from sickness due to the overcrowding and promoted idleness. The only time the large French crews might enjoy an advantage was in the event of a boarding action, but only if the men had not succumbed to illness first.

Miniature portrait of an *Aspirant de Marine* in 1800. Replacing the *Gardes de la Marines* in 1786, the post became open to elite, wealthy families from outside the nobility. After the Revolution this path to the rank of *ensigne* was also opened to ship's boys who showed promise in the lessons.

The ship's officers

Since 1765 an officer could only attain the rank of *capitaine de vaisseau* after a long career in which he had acquired the instruction and experience necessary to command a battleship. When applied to the commander of a ship of the line, the term 'captain' is somewhat misleading. The rank of *capitaine de vaisseau* was in fact equivalent to an army colonel. He would have spent at least 18 months with a sea command at the rank of *capitaine de frégate* (frigate captain, or commander) in which he had fulfilled important missions and shown bravery in action. Previous to that he would have spent at least two years with the rank of lieutenant, a grade he would have attained only after serving two years as an *ensigne*.

The rank of *ensigne* could be achieved by two separate routes. The traditional route had been through the *Gardes de la Marine* and *Gardes du Pavillon*. Admission to the *gardes* was open only to members of the nobility who were able to obtain a letter of appointment, thus favouring sons of existing naval officers. With more emphasis on theoretical training than the practical experience given to British midshipmen, by the 1780s the *gardes* were by reputation arrogant, unruly and even violent. In 1786 the *gardes* were disbanded and replaced by officer *aspirants*. Two schools opened in Vannes and Alais offering places to these *aspirants* who could now come from outside the nobility, albeit only from rich families. The courses offered were based more on practical seamanship, but before any changes could be realized, the schools were shut down on 15 May 1791 and were not replaced until 22 October 1795 when new ones were opened in Brest, Toulon and Rochefort.

The second route to *ensigne* was open to *capitaines de commerce* from the merchant fleet. A merchant captain needed to have five years' experience at sea and to pass a public exam before being accepted. These officers *non-entretenue* (better known as *officiers bleues* before the Revolution) were the object of considerable disdain by the so-called *Grand Corps*, the aristocrat-dominated officer elite.

The Revolution, with its *Declaration of the Rights of Man*, terminally shattered the concept of authority based on aristocratic privilege. Officers of the *Grand Corps* began to meet with previously unimaginable acts of insubordination, often stoked by militant dockworkers and politically charged civilians. Why was such-and-such a command being given? On what authority was the command given? Did it run contrary to the principles of the Revolution? No longer able to fulfil their commissions, many also fearing for their personal security, the *Grand Corps* fled France in droves.

Unfortunately for the new order, the loss of so many experienced naval officers (on 1 May 1791 there were only 42 out of 170 captains remaining) left a gaping hole at the top that needed to be filled. To make up the deficiency, an appeal went out to retired officers, commercial captains and harbour

II. RANK EQUIVALENTS 25th OCTOBER 1795	
NAVY	**ARMY**
Capitaine de vaisseau	Colonel
Capitaine de frégate	Chef de bataillon
Lieutenant de vaisseau	Capitaine
Enseigne de vaisseau	Lieutenant
Premier maître	Sergent-major
Second maître	Sergent
Contre maître	Caporal-fourrier
Quartier maître	Caporal
Gabier, matelot	Soldier
Mousse	Enfant de troupe

Capitaine de Vaisseau, **engraving by Labrousse. Notice the pistols worn in the sash.**

pilots, and the advancement of *lieutenants de vaisseau* was accelerated. In a further move to increase the numbers of officers, a tenth of all *ensigne* places were given over to masters and helmsmen, thus opening an important promotional route to senior crewmen. However, these stopgap measures inevitably led to a drop in quality. Commanding a commercial vessel was an inadequate preparation for a battleship captain who, as well as being an excellent mariner, needed the instincts of a warrior if he was to succeed.

Masters and idlers

The most experienced sailors on each ship were the *officiers-mariniers*, who executed the commands of the ship's officers. The most senior officer-mariner was the *maître d'equipage*, or more simply 'the Master'. With authority over the crew, the Master directed the manoeuvre of the vessel under the orders of the captain, or watch officer. Typically the Master's orders were transmitted by means of a silver *sifflet* (a call, or whistle) carried in his tunic buttonhole. With a varying pitch, each call relayed different orders, which were acknowledged by the crewmen with a shout of '*Commande!*'

Capitaine de Vaisseau, **by Vernet-Lamy. This officer is wearing the ribbon of the legion of honour, signifying it is from after 1802.**

The *maître d'equipage* was the most senior of the *maîtres de manoeuvre*, a group including the Master, a Second Master, the Master's Mates, a *bosseman* (a corruption of the English 'boatswain', but principally in charge of anchors and the matelots working on the forecastle), quartermasters and the coxen (coxswain) of the ship's boats. Collectively they were responsible for distributing tasks to matelots, as well as maintaining the ropes, cables, pulleys, shackles and anchors. The *maîtres de manoeuvre* were drawn from first-class matelots with at least six months' experience working as a *gabiers* (top-men). Alternatively, they could have spent two long-haul voyages on a merchantman with the rank of *maître d'equipage*.

The *maîtres de canonnage* (master gunners) were drawn from men who had studied in one of the artillery schools and had served 12 months with the gun teams on a warship or as a matelot for 24 months. The position was also open to sailors who had been at sea for four years, with half that time spent as an artillery servant. It was not uncommon for Marine artillerymen from the ship's garrison to fulfil the role of master gunner to supplement their pay. As a distinctive mark these soldiers would wear a gold stripe around the collar of their coats. Those that obtained 'the merit of Second Master' wore a woollen stripe coloured *aurora* (light orange).

The master gunner was responsible for making up the gun crews and ensuring they were properly trained. He also ensured that the regulation number of cannonballs and cartridge bags were embarked and correctly stored with the proper instruments (see Plate A). The

Sailors rowing officers to a frigate. Notice the billhook carried by the sailor at the front. A *maître de manoeuvre* can be seen on the tiller, wearing a sidearm.

master gunner was also in command of the *capitaine d'armes*, a position traditionally filled by a Marine infantry sergeant. He would look after all the small arms, muskets, pistols, pikes and boarding axes, distributing them to soldiers and sailors prior to combat. He also retained the key to the arms chests placed on the quarterdeck.

Next came the *maîtres de timonerie* (helmsmen), the most junior of whom required 24 months' experience of navigation, including six months on the helm, before being selected. In addition to steering the ship they were expected to check the condition of the rudder and compasses, maintain the logs and journals, as well as the signals and lamps. They worked closely with the *pilotes-cotiers* (harbour pilots) who were put on board for their special knowledge of certain areas of coastline or ocean important to the particular voyage being undertaken. In battle the two most senior helmsmen (one from each watch) would be placed at the ship's wheel.

There were three principal types of artificers on board, including the *maîtres de charpentage* (shipwrights), *de calfatage* (caulkers) and *de voilerie* (sail-makers). In addition to 12 months at sea, each master artificer would have spent at least three years practising his trade in the ports and arsenals. The shipwrights would ensure enough tools, planks and spars were embarked to make running repairs to the ship and its mast. The caulkers would carry bitumen and pitch for tarring. Typically the caulkers would use an iron spike and a mallet for hammering caulking (a packing material made from hemp and old rope), to seal any leaks or holes. The master caulkers were also responsible for maintaining the ship's pumps. In combat the caulkers occupied one of the most perilous stations. On the *faux pont* (orlop deck) was a narrow gallery that went around the edge of the ship (the 'carpenters' walk' on British ships), which was stocked with wooden plugs, tallow and lead plates. When cannonballs began striking the hull and making holes on or around the waterline, the caulkers would have to pass through this gallery and repair the damage.

In addition to these officer-mariners there were a number of 'non-officer-mariners' or supernumeraries, including blacksmiths, coppersmiths and armourers. These supernumeraries were commonly known as '*les fainéants*' (idlers) as they did not make up part of the watches at sea. Surgeons and an apothecary to supply medicines also numbered among the idlers, along with a number of men put on board to help the steward distribute the rations, including victuallers, cooks, butchers, bakers and coopers. Finally, there were a number of domestic staff for the officers, sailors no longer being used as servants since the Revolution.

III. CREW COMPOSITION 3 Brumaire Year IV (25th October 1795)		SHIP TYPE			
		118	110	80	74
État-major	Capitaine de vaisseaux	1	1	1	1
	Capitaine de frégate	1	1	1	1
	Lieutenants de vaisseaux	6	6	5	4
	Ensigns de vaisseaux	9	9	7	7
	Officers of the Garrison	2	2	1	1
	Commissaries (Pursers)	1	1	1	1
	Chief Medical Officers	1	1	1	1
	Aspirants	9	9	9	7
Officer-mariners	Manoeuvre First-masters 1st, 2nd & 3rd class	2	2	2	2
	Second-masters 1st & 2nd class	3	3	2	2
	Contre-masters 1st & 2nd class	4	4	3	3
	Quarter-masters 1st, 2nd & 3rd class	24	24	18	16
	Gunners Masters 1st & 2nd class	4	4	3	3
	Seconds-masters 1st, 2nd & 3rd class	7	7	4	4
	Gunners mates 1st, 2nd & 3rd class	66	62	48	42
	Helmsmen Masters 1st, 2nd & 3rd class	2	2	2	2
	Second-masters 1st, 2nd & 3rd class	6	6	5	4
	Mates 1st, 2nd & 3rd class	10	10	8	7
	Harbour Pilots	2	2	1	1
Officer-mariners	Shipwrights Masters 1st, 2nd & 3rd class	1	1	1	1
	Seconds-masters 1st, 2nd & 3rd class	2	2	2	1
	Mates 1st, 2nd, 3rd & 4th class	5	5	5	3
	Caulkers Masters 1st, 2nd & 3rd class	1	1	1	1
	Seconds-masters 1st, 2nd & 3rd class	2	2	2	1
	Mates 1st, 2nd, 3rd & 4th class	6	5	5	3
	Sail makers Masters 1st, 2nd & 3rd class	1	1	1	1
	Seconds-masters 1st, 2nd & 3rd class	1	1	1	1
	Mates 1st, 2nd, 3rd & 4th class	3	3	2	2
Supernumeraries	Matelots 1st class	121	114	95	76
	2nd class	121	114	95	76
	3rd class	121	114	95	76
	4th class	121	114	95	76
	Novices 1st & 2nd class	161	150	125	101
	Mousses (boys) 1st & 2nd class	80	75	60	50
	Soldiers of the garrison (includes artillerymen)	180	170	130	100
	Armourers Premiers – 1st, 2nd & 3rd class	1	1	1	1
	Seconds – 1st, 2nd & 3rd class	1	1	1	1
	Blacksmiths 1st, 2nd & 3rd class	2	2	-	-
	Coppersmiths 1st, 2nd & 3rd class	1	1	-	-
	Victuallers 1st & 2nd class	1	1	-	-
	Surgeons Seconds	2	2	2	2
	Surgeon's mates	4	4	2	2
	Apothecaries (Chemists)	1	1	1	1
	Employees of rations. Premier Stewards	1	2	1	1
	Second Stewards	3	2	2	1
	Ration Distributors	2	2	2	2
	Cooks	2	2	1	1
	Butchers	1	1	1	1
	Bakers	1	1	1	1
	Coopers 1st & 2nd class	2	2	1	1
	Orderlies for officers	17	17	13	13
	GRAND TOTALS:	**1130**	**1070**	**866**	**706**

Sea wolves and freshwater matelots

The bulk of the crew comprised matelots and novices. Matelots were classed according to their length of service – a first-class sailor would normally have spent four years as a fully fledged matelot. Such an experienced seaman was known as a *loup de mer* (sea wolf), while novices were known by the derogatory title of *matelots d'eau douce* (freshwater sailors).

The elite matelots were designated *gabiers*, who worked aloft on the masts, hoisting, lowering and adjusting the sails. Other matelots worked as assistants to the shipwrights, caulkers, armourers and sail-makers, perhaps aspiring to one day becoming a master artificer in their own right. The *prévôt d'equipage* on the other hand was the derogatory name

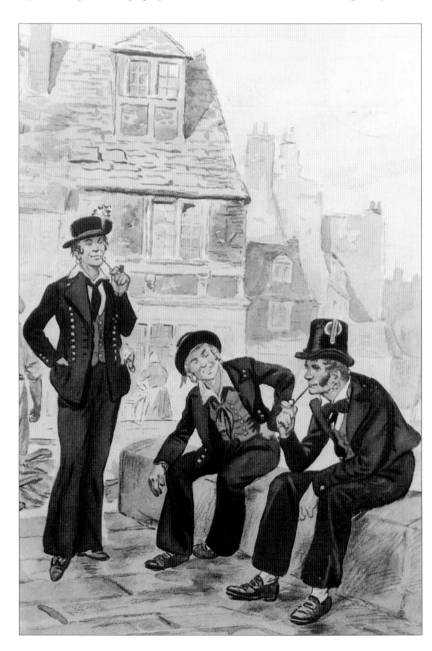

Sailors on shore in full dress. Garneray provides a very different description of their costume: 'His costume, of a deplorable maturity, shone more from the tar than from cleanliness. A beggar would have scorned to pick it up.'

jokingly given to the most incompetent, useless man on the ship. In former days the *prévôt* was responsible for inflicting punishments, but by the end of the 1790s the titleholder was limited to sweeping-up and other cleaning duties, with boys or other juveniles often detailed to help by way of a punishment.

Some memoirs show that novices were bullied by the more experienced sailors. Joining a ship in Toulon, the Parisian volunteer Sanglé-Ferrière was singled out:

> I found it humiliating to be confused with this band of rogues, the majority in rags and whose language reflected their villainous origin. They only spoke the Provençal dialect and as I was ignorant in my new profession, I appeared stupid to them and became the object of their jokes. Our chief helmsman was a brutal former revolutionary from Marseilles, where he had figured as an ardent Jacobin. He was named Quesnel and took a hatred of me, because, wearing a tailed coat, he supposed me an aristocrat. I feared his terrible *garcette* (a length of braided rope and old yarn) more than death and I could see that this malicious man burned with desire to hit me with it.

The ship's boys

The last group of sailors were the *mousses*, the ship's boys, who were expected to grow up at sea and become the matelots of the future. Their title was derived from the Spanish '*moço*' (snot) and there were approximately one for every ten crewmen. The *mousses* were divided into two classes, a first-class *mousse* being a boy aged over 13 with 18 months at sea. At 16 the *mousse* would become a novice until physically developed enough to be recognized as a fully fledged matelot.

Under the *ancien régime* boys received schooling from the ship's chaplain, but with Christianity suppressed during the Revolution this practice was no longer possible. Instead, on 4 February 1794 the government decreed that all ships with 20 guns or more would employ an *instituteur* (tutor) to teach 'the young citizens on board'. Lessons would comprise reading, writing, calculation and 'the first elements of navigational theory'. In keeping with the times, there were incessant readings of *The Declaration of the Rights of Man* and of the Constitution, albeit in simple, easily explained terms. Finally, the students would be taught history, with the tutor advised to concentrate on the 'actions of the defenders of Liberty', i.e. the armies fighting on the land frontiers. Lessons would be held twice a day at a time and place of the captain's choosing. In addition to the boys and novices under the age of 18, these lessons were open to all members of the crew that might find themselves off duty at lesson time.

The tutors would be paid by the state and would be chosen by a council composed of the captain, first-lieutenant, the Master and three matelots who were fathers. He would 'mess' with the *état-major* and was monitored by the first-lieutenant, who ensured that he fulfilled his teaching duties properly. If he was found lacking he was to be denounced and publicly censured before the assembled crew, then reported to the Naval Ministry on return to port, whereupon he would be dismissed and banned from serving on any of the Republic's warships.

Any boys that revealed a talent during their schooling were to be singled out as being capable of 'serving the Homeland in more elevated ranks'. At the end of the campaign at sea they were to receive a certificate from the ship's officers and sit an exam. Those that succeeded would be admitted to the rank of *éleves de la marine* (naval pupils) from where they could aspire to become officers. This practice was continued by Napoleon, who stipulated that once a boy had been at sea for six months and if he passed an examination, he could become an *aspirant* 'of the lowest class'.

Although *mousses* were most often the sons of sailors, there are examples of boys being recruited from outside the maritime communities. Auguste Gicquel's elder brother had already joined the navy when in the spring of 1794 he and another brother were targeted by recruiters in Paris:

> One day while Olivier and myself played with the other kids our age, a recruiting sergeant passed by, who gained our confidence. He proposed to employ us against the English, and for this reason was going to enrol us in the navy at Brest, which was, according to him, the most tempting of trades. We were too well prepared by the stories of our brother not to let ourselves be easily convinced, and the idea of making war against the English finally decided us.

At the time, Gicquel was just nine and his brother 11 years old.

The ship's garrison

Every ship had a garrison of Marine troops who, unlike the sailors drawn from the maritime classes, were full-time professional soldiers. Their primary functions were to provide a corps of artillery specialists, keep order among the crew and to form landing parties. On 14 June 1792, four regiments of Marine infantry and two regiments of Marine artillery

Soldiers from infantry regiments often made up significant parts of the ship's garrison; however, it was recognized that specialist troops were better used to the rigours onboard.

were created to replace the Royal Corps of *cannoniers-matelots*, which had fulfilled this role since 1786. However, after some of these troops fought against the Republican government at the siege of Toulon, the government abolished the regiments (28 January 1794). Army infantrymen were given crash courses in naval gunnery and then put on ships as replacements. On 25 October 1795, the government again recognized the need for specialist Marine gunners and so created seven *demi-brigades* of Marine artillery. Three of these *demi-brigades* were based at Brest, one at Lorient, one at Rochefort and two at Toulon. With no specific infantry component, the gunners would also provide the ship's garrison, often with the assistance of army infantrymen.

On 5 May 1803, the seven *demi-brigades* were consolidated into six regiments of Marine artillery. These troops were recruited by voluntary engagement from 'robust' and 'healthy' men between 16 and 30 years of age, at least 5ft 5in in height. The duration of engagement would be for eight years, at the expiration of which the men could re-enlist for additional four-year periods of service.

Despite these changes in organization, the function of the ship's garrison remained fairly constant throughout the period. When not at sea, the Marine troops were charged with the security of the ports, arsenals and coastal batteries. In the arsenals they were responsible for constructing specialist artillery ammunition (canister, grape and bar shot), as well as the loading, unloading and storage of weapons, ammunition and gun tools. The gunners were frequently drilled in loading cannons, either on the land batteries or onboard special boats laid out for this purpose in the harbour. Napoleon ordered that gunners successfully striking a target were to be paid a gratification. All Marine troops were also instructed in standard infantry drill and were armed with an artillery-pattern musket and bayonet (see Plate A).

Marine officers made up an important part of the ship's *état-major* and were subordinate to the ship's captain and his second in command. The senior officer took charge of the artillery and concerned himself with every facet of the guns, their equipment and the munitions onboard. He was responsible to the ship's captain for the correct loading of ordnance on the ship, visiting the *sainte-barbe* (gun room), powder stores and chests, the wells and floors where the cannonballs were stored, the hooks, rings and shutters of the gun ports. He would take the ship's master gunner with him on this inspection, in which he would note down the weights, numbers, foundry marks and the lengths of each artillery piece. If any failings were recorded, this officer would report to the second in command.

While at sea the officer would make weekly inspections of all the weapons on board. Each evening he would make a tour of the batteries ensuring everything was correct. When in sight of the enemy he would make a final inspection of the batteries and inform the captain when everything was ready for action. In combat, the senior artillery officer did not have a fixed position – he was to be near to the captain and carried himself as directed. He was not to give any direct orders to the gunners, only to transmit those of the captain to the officers posted at the batteries and to alert the captain of any problems he could perceive. The other garrison officers were divided between the service of the batteries and directing musketry, as ordered by the ship's captain.

LIFE AT SEA

Due to the limited space, an enormous amount of organization went into managing the crew's actions. A list was drawn up by the first-lieutenant called the *rôle des quarts* (watch bill), which was fixed to a plank at the entrance of the poop deck. This list divided the crew into two *bordées* (watches): the first, or *quart de tribord* (the starboard watch) and the second, the *quart de basbord* (the larboard watch).

The men of the duty *quart* would perform the duties of manoeuvring the vessel while the rest of the crew would sleep or enjoy periods of recreation. 'All hands' would only be called together when the ship was being washed down each morning and during combat drills or battle. A ship with its crew divided into two watches was said to be running the *grande bordée* or 'sea watch'. However, in port the captain could opt to run the ship with an additional third *quart* to offer more leisure time.

The ship's day began at midday when the sun was observed and the vessel's true latitude could be correctly ascertained. Lescallier's 1798 *Maritime Vocabulary* describes how the day at sea was divided into six four-hour watches, with each watch being broken down into eight half-hour periods. However, to prevent men from serving the same hours of watch every day, the 'evening watch' (4–8pm) was cut in half (see Table IV).

Time was measured by an *ampoulette* (sand-glass) and on every half-hour, when the *ampoulette* was turned, the helmsman would order the smaller of the two ship's bells to be rung, calling out, for example, '*pique trois*' ('strike three') on the passage of the third half-hour of the watch. The helmsman would also announce the end of the watch (accompanied by the ringing of the ship's larger bell) and call up the next watch with the cry of '*quart de basbord*' or '*tribord*' as applicable. To let the two duty officers (the *officiers de quart*) know they were still alert, the night watches would respond to the ringing of the half-hour bell with the call of '*à l'autre bon quart*' ('all's well').

Living conditions

It is perhaps very difficult to comprehend the living conditions on board a damp, dimly lit, rolling and pitching, overcrowded, wooden warship at the end of the 18th century. As soon as a voyage began, rain and seawater would begin to collect at the bottom of the hold where it stagnated in the ballast, filling the ship with a putrid air. This water teemed with disease-carrying mosquito larvae and the carcasses of dead rats. Unwashed sailors' bodies and clothes were infested with parasitical lice and fleas. The reek of manure and urine from the animals in the manger would waft through the ship. For ships operating in tropical climes, an oppressive stench rose up from below decks and bordered on the unbearable.

Entering this world for the first time, Garneray, a depressed novice, wrote:

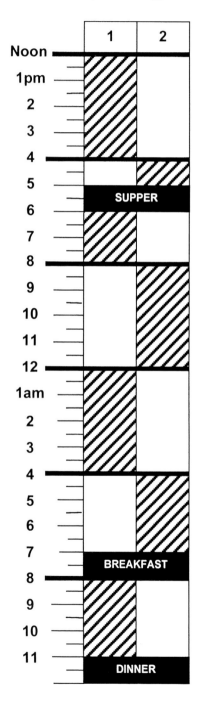

Table IV: the rotation of watches over a two-day period at sea. Notice how a sailor would be on duty (shaded areas) 14 hours the first day, but only ten the next. Meal times could vary, but this example dates from the expedition to Egypt.

The spectacle which presented itself was so far from the idea that I had formed of a ship that for a moment I remained totally stunned and dared not believe the testimony of my eyes. Instead of those vain sailors, quarter-masters and officers, dressed in the brilliant uniforms that my imagination had unceasingly dreamt of for such a long time, I saw only dirty people, slovenly, covered with poor, wretched rags, resembling pirates or bandits rather than servants of the State. The cleanliness of the ship also left much to be desired.

The men slept on *hamacs* (trad-itionally called *branles*), which were made from a piece of canvas 6ft long by 4ft or 5ft wide. The ends of the hammock had a series of eyelets through which ropes were attached to the beams in the deck-head over the cannons. There was space for 318 tightly packed hammocks on the main deck of a 74-gun ship, which meant that only one *bordée* could sleep at a time. The traditional French practice was for men from different watches to use the same hammock, but after 4 February 1794 each sailor was issued with his own, a measure that unwittingly helped prevent the spread of disease between men.

The ship's officers did not fare much better. The captain was accorded the luxury of a cabin at the rear of the ship, but the other officers slung their cots (*hamacs à l'Anglais*) in temporary compartments formed by hanging wooden partitions or canvas screens in the space between two cannons. Any private possessions were stored in a sea chest, which, perhaps with the addition of a folding stool, would be stored under the cot while he slept.

In an attempt to maintain the health of those on board, a number of precautions were built into the daily routine. Maintaining fresh air circulation was considered vitally important, so each morning the gun ports were opened to air the lower decks. Each matelot would wash his mouth out with water and vinegar, before taking his kitbag, hammock and blanket up on to deck, where they were beaten and exposed to the air for at least two hours. The urinals, which were at the side of the ship to the rear of the foremast, were to be cleaned every day. Laundry was done on the 15th and 30th of each month, the dirty articles put into tubs on deck and washed in boiling water mixed with cinders.

Chef d'escadre (chief of naval squadron) in service uniform, (tricolour sash, white collar and cuff flaps, red breeches and cuffs, gold embroidery) by Labrousse. Notice the furniture that would have formed part of the ship's *grand chambre*.

The kitchen area was located on the upper deck to the rear of the foremast. It consisted of an oven and a separate large, square stove, bordered by thick planks that were held in place by metal uprights with a masonry floor at the base. The cooking surface was divided into two sections by a stanchion, one side being for the crew's food, the other for the officers'. The crew's meals were cooked in a large 720-litre copper vessel, while the officers' pots and pans were placed on an iron grill. Smoke from the kitchens escaped through a chimney rising out through the forecastle deck, next to which were placed buckets of water in case of fire.

Meals were eaten next to the guns in messes of seven men, with soup served communally in a shallow wooden bowl called a *gamelle*. The men would sit on the deck round the bowl and each take it in turns for a spoonful. Sailors had notoriously bad teeth because of the effects of scurvy (vitamin C deficiency), so many would be forced to dunk their hard, double-cooked *galettes* (biscuits) into the soup before attempting to eat them. The wine ration was served in a communal pot called a *bidon* (see Plate H). The ship's officers would each contribute to a communal mess bill, part of which would go directly to the cook for their share of the normal rations, the rest for additional items.

Rations and stowage

According to the law of 30 June 1798, each man, regardless of rank, was to receive a daily ration that included 24 French ounces of fresh bread (half a loaf) or 18 ounces of biscuit (three biscuits, each 7–7½in. in diameter). Each man also received a pint of red wine from the Bordeaux or Lower Languedoc regions, with those from Saintonge, Anjou and Touraine acceptable for voyages under a month in duration. If operating out of the Channel ports, Belgium or Holland, the wine could be substituted for 1½ pints beer or cider, which was considerably less than the 8 pints received daily by British sailors.

Dinners were varied over the course of each *décade* – the ten-day week in the Revolutionary calendar. On days one, four, six and eight of each *décade* the men were served 4oz of salted cod seasoned with olive oil and vinegar. An 8oz portion of beef was served twice a *décade*, with salt pork on the remaining days. For supper, each man would be provided with 4oz of peas, beans or 2oz of rice, seasoned with salt, olive oil and vinegar. After six or seven weeks at sea it was expected that both the cod and the beef would no longer be fit for consumption, so all meals would include salt pork. If the cod ran out earlier than expected, it would be replaced with a ration of 3oz Gruyère or Dutch cheese, or 4oz of vegetables, including dried peas and beans.

When possible these basic rations would be supplemented with fresh green vegetables and dried tablets of bouillon (stock). The ship was also packed with 2lb 8oz of mustard grain, 130lb of salt and 7 pints of vinegar (to mix with the water and to prepare the mustard) per 100 men, per month, along with ½oz of pepper per 100 rations.

Some livestock was normally embarked for ocean voyages, including up to six cattle and 20 chickens per 100 men. The chickens were kept in poultry cages on the poop deck while the cattle were herded into a manger forward of the kitchen on the upper deck. The chickens were often replaced with ducks, geese or turkeys, as chickens had an unfortunate habit of dying from seasickness. To feed the livestock, 400lb of hay per cow and 18lb of small grain per chicken were embarked.

Additional rations were stored for the exclusive use of the sick and wounded, including four to eight sheep (plus 50lb hay each), 20 bouillon tablets, 10lb butter, 20lb raisins, 40lb prunes, 8lb sugar, ½oz sorrel conserve and 1oz pickled cabbage (sauerkraut).

A ship would stock as much as three months' drinking water in the hold. The drinking water was placed on the deck in scuttlebutts set either side of the main mast and was drunk from a communal horn. If stale, the water was mixed with vinegar, or if scurvy was present, with vinegar and a little *eau-de-vie* (brandy). In hot climates, the water was mixed with *eau-de-vie*, lemons and sugar. However, a common problem recorded by Garneray was that 'the rats in the hold had pierced a great number of the water barrels.'

To provide these rations for the crew an enormous amount of supplies and munitions were embarked at the beginning of each voyage. The ship would have to carry all the utensils necessary for preparing and serving dinner for the entire crew, not to mention enough fuel for cooking over the length of the journey. The quantities of foodstuffs packed on board were equally staggering. For example, on one of the gigantic three-deckers, six months of rations would include 325,415 pints of wine, 190,331lb biscuit, 90,807lb flour, 46,970lb salt pork, 3,872lb salt beef, 4,528lb cod, 6,791lb cheese, 6,145lb vegetables, 4,528lb rice, 15,523lb peas, 15,523lb beans, 15,523lb broad beans, 3,557lb oil, 10,069lb vinegar, 9,702lb salt, 107lb mustard and 548lb candles.

A naval *Commissaire Ordonnateur de Guerres* was responsible for supplying ships at the beginning of a voyage. (Engraving by Labrousse)

The actual *arrimage* (stowage) was organized by the first-lieutenant. This exercise was extremely important as even the best ships would handle badly if incorrectly balanced. The lieutenant would draw up a chart showing how the weight would be distributed evenly throughout the hold. The first thing to be loaded would be the ship's ballast, which consisted of irons bars arranged in equal quantity on each side of the ship to provide it with stability. Shingle was then tipped over the ballast and levelled off. The first level of water and wine barrels were laid into the shingle with logs inserted between them to prevent them rolling. A second layer of barrels was placed on top, then a third level consisting of provisions like salt, vinegar, charcoal, salt-meats, cod, olive oil, lamp oil, tar and so forth. These three levels of stores did not extend into the extremities of the hold fore and aft, which were reserved for bread and the gunpowder barrels, not to mention spare parts and equipment for the artificers. The forward area was reserved for the anchor cables, ropes and hawsers. Finally, around the sides of the orlop deck there were additional storage compartments called *soutes* where vegetables, provisions for the captain's table and other miscellaneous objects were stored.

However, before anything was loaded onto the ship, a *conseil de salubrité* (board of health), formed by the first-lieutenant, the chief medical officer and the purser, would first inspect the ship and have the hold cleared, washed and 'purified' with hydrochloric acid, then whitened with chalk. A second commission, formed by the ship's commander, several officers from the staff and again the purser, would then inspect the quality and quantity of foodstuffs provided by the port authorities to ensure they were fit for consumption. This did not prevent, soon after loading, the hold being filled with rats gnawing their way through the water barrels or boxes of already maggot-infested biscuits being stowed aboard.

Combat stations, drills and seamanship

At the beginning of each voyage a *rôle de combat* was drawn up detailing each crewman to a particular battle station. A large number of men were required to serve the guns, both as specialists and as 'servants' to haul them back into the firing position after loading. A 36-pounder (each piece weighed over 3 tons) officially required a crew of 15 men. However, each gun crew was responsible for both the starboard and larboard gun in their battery. Ideally the ship would only be engaged on one side at a time, but if necessary, the crew could operate the pair simultaneously. The specialists would remain at the individual guns while the servants alternated between guns to 'run them out' after loading. In addition, two men from each gun crew (one from the smaller 12-pounders) would be nominated as 'boarders'.

All good captains knew the importance of preparing their crews for combat through frequent drills. Therefore gunners would run through artillery drills

Grenades were most effective when dropped from the rigging onto crowded enemy decks below. If an enemy crew sheltered below decks, shipwrights would stave open the decks to allow grenades to be dropped into the ship's interior.

while those designated as boarders would practise their weaponry. Soldiers would spend time firing muskets from the 'tops' (platforms in the masts) and grenade men would practise throwing grenades using papier-mâché models. The most pressing exercise, however, was learning the complex procedure of preparing the ship for combat.

Before a ship went into action a huge number of tasks had to be performed in preparation. Captains would train their crews in making '*branles-bas*' ('hammocks down') which meant clearing the decks for action. Hammocks were rolled and taken up on deck and packed in the nets along the side of the ship where, along with the men's kitbags filled with their *hardes* (clothes), they would offer some protection against enemy musketry and canister fire. To further protect those on deck, large nets were put up and extra lashings were added to the yards and blocks to prevent them falling.

Nothing could be allowed to impede the loading of the guns, so all the partitions between the officers' quarters were dismantled and their personal effects bundled into the hold without ceremony. The orlop deck was cleared and made ready to receive the wounded. A table was set up to hold all the surgeon's implements and a number of matelots were detailed to carry the wounded. The boxes of small arms and grenades were brought up on deck and distributed by the captain of arms to the boarders who would keep them at their regular station until called for. Sacks of cartridges were brought forward and temporary shot-parks created to place the cannonballs nearer the guns. Rope

The bare-chested sailor is levering up the barrel so that the man aiming the piece can elevate or decrease the barrel by means of the wooden wedge. Notice the powder horn worn over his shoulder used for priming the gun after loading.

V. CANNON STATISTICS				
Weight of Shot*	Metric (kilos)	Diameter of Ball	Cal. of Barrel	Weight of Cannon
36 (39)	17.622kg	168mm	175mm	3516.95kg
24 (26)	11.748kg	147mm	152mm	2502.47kg
18 (19)	8.811kg	134mm	139mm	2060.27kg
12 (13)	5.874kg	117mm	121mm	1464.98kg
8 (8½)	3.916kg	103mm	106mm	1173.96kg
6 (6½)	2.937kg	93mm	96mm	847.69kg

*In French Pounds (British equivalent shown in brackets)

VI. PENETRATION OF SOLID OAK						
Gun Type	Powder Charge	RANGE AT 0° ELEVATION				
		100m	200m	400m	600m	1000m
36	6kg	1.3m	1.2m	1m	0.9m	0.65m
18	3kg	1.1m	1m	0.8m	0.6m	0.4m
8	1.5kg	0.9cm	0.8m	0.65m	0.49m	0.27m

This chart demonstrates the destructive potential of French naval artillery. It is sobering to think that the maximum hull thickness of a 74-gun ship was just 80cm.

curtains were put up in gun decks to protect the crews from flying splinters, while tubs and buckets of water would be positioned around the gun in case of fire. If the engagement was likely to go on past nightfall, tin 'battle lanterns' were hung on sockets in between every other cannon to illuminate the gun decks.

While these drills progressed, the complex business of sailing the ship took place. For *aspirants* and novices it would take years to learn, not just the handling of the ship, but the vocabulary of specialist nautical terms. A good matelot was expected to know how to work and arrange the rigging, to know the names of all the ropes on the ship, to make all the different knots used in the navy, all the splices, how to strap and to strike the pulleys, to unbend the sails from their yards, deploy and orientate them, to furl them, to make repairs to sails cut in combat or torn by high winds, how to work the anchors, to move and secure them, to load and unload stores, to steer and take soundings.

Aspirant Gicquel was fortunate to have the help of his elder brother (a *lieutenant de vaisseau*) when learning his trade:

> He continued to give me lessons of astronomy and mathematics, to teach me the problems of navigation, and initiated me into the thousand details of our profession. Each time a delicate or perilous operation was carried out in the masts, he made me come up on deck, indicating to me the precautions to be taken, explaining the reasons for them.

Without detailed navigational charts, ship's captains were heavily reliant on the experienced harbour pilots when operating close to the coast or when entering a port. Moreau de Jonnes described a Breton pilot who came onboard, attributing his navigational prowess to mystical origins:

> He inspected the frigate's sail with a sneer, made certain alterations, and caused screens to be placed over the helmsmens' lanterns, whose light incommoded him. He took his place beside the captain, who used his authority to carry out the orders he prescribed. This man, whose commands dominated us like Destiny, was a pilot from lower Brittany, the type of sailor that can neither read nor write but has inherited the experience transmitted from father to son in each family since the boatmen of the Veneti guided the fleets of Rome some twenty centuries ago. A peculiarity which struck our men and gave rise to superstition was the fact that this pilot could see in the darkest night, and that he consulted the deepest shadow when steering

the frigate amongst the reefs; and it was a fact that his eyes remained fixed on points of the horizon where we could not discover the slightest glimmer, and seemed to find there the elements necessary to guide us. I often thought that some distant light must serve him as a guide; but none among us could make out anything of the kind, and the crew came to the conclusion that the pilot was endowed with second sight.

Garneray received a rude introduction to what he called 'maritime gymnastics'. With the pitching of the vessel in strong winds, the work of the *gabiers* was typically nerve-wracking for the uninitiated:

> That which they call the *marchepied* is in fact a rope of medium thickness, attached to the middle and the end of a yardarm, on which you balance in thin air. Seeing myself thus suspended almost eighty feet above a furious sea, which dashed the frigate as if it had been a stick of straw, I felt myself taken with giddiness, and I clung on as best I could.

Sanglé-Ferrière experienced similar difficulties and found himself in need of rescue when paralysed with fear:

> Following me was an old Genoese sailor who realized my sufferings and generously came to my assistance. He passed around my back and helped me with one hand, while he supported us with the other. It took three hours to exchange that wretched sail; one can imagine my torment during this time!

Sailors that performed their duties in rain or heavy seas were allowed a shot of *eau-de-vie* (one bottle between 32 men) at the end of their watch. When they returned to their hammocks, carefully placed lanterns could be lit in the sleeping area while the men changed into dry clothes. As a precaution, a lieutenant would inspect the lanterns and make sure that none of the sailors had gone to sleep in wet clothes.

Collisions with other ships, reefs or bad weather could cripple a ship and the ability to make running repairs was vital although often hazardous. Surgeon-Major Félix Charyau was off the African coast when his ship lost its rudder:

> All the hinges were broken and the helm broken off. The hinges were remade but the old fittings prevented the new ones being put in place. One of our gunners offered to dive in and take them out. This enterprise was hazardous, for the sight of sharks surrounding our frigate gave some anxiety. This courageous man passed a rope around his body under the arms and threw himself into the water, then went in search of the rudder's fittings. Several times we were compelled to pull him out promptly because of the sharks.

Battling boredom

All too often life at sea was tedious and dull. As part of the ship's garrison, Moreau de Jonnes quickly grew bored with it:

Astounded at this monotony I complained bitterly, but the old sailors told me that it was often thus; that there were men who had sailed for fifty years without having seen a single bad storm, and others who had served the ten campaigns of the American War without having seen a single naval battle.

To alleviate boredom and the onset of depression (often an early symptom of scurvy), music and games were encouraged. As Surgeon Charyau confirms: 'To beat the boredom we had a man named Mazeau from Nantes who played the clarinet passably well. We played music every evening.' The regulations encouraged officers to excite their crew with games and dances, embarking an accordion where possible, because 'gaiety is one of the best means to keep the men healthy and ward off scurvy.'

French sailors from the Atlantic coast amused themselves with popular songs called *rondes du bord* (ring dances), which were often accompanied by bagpipes and Breton-style dancing. Sailors from the Mediterranean ports, on the other hand, were more likely to use flutes and tambourines for accompaniment. Unfortunately not much is known about French sailors' songs from the period. In general they were divided into bawdy, popular tunes and 'working songs' used to unite the actions of sailors hauling ropes or working the capstans. With these songs the verse was sung by one sailor and then repeated by a chorus of the others.

In addition to songs, music-playing and telling yarns, the men also played dice, cards, dominoes, draughts (chequers), quoits with rope rings and, according to Moreau de Jonnes, backgammon. Crews also celebrated crossing the equator with a *baptisme*, which Lescallier described as a 'ridiculous ceremony, but very old among men of the sea, which consists of ducking those passing the equinoctial line for the first time.' The ceremony had its origins in passing the tropics or a notable sea passage like the Straits of Gibraltar and was celebrated by crews on

Sailors dancing to the accompaniment of an accordion and fiddle. Music played a vital role in keeping up morale during long sea voyages.

Napoleon gives a snuff to a sailor. Smoking restrictions on board ship meant that tobacco was more often chewed. (Dubreuil)

the expedition to Egypt in 1798, principally as a means to extract money out of their passengers.[1]

It was standard for 3lb of tobacco to be issued to each man at the beginning of a voyage. However, with the ever-present fear of fire, smoking was tightly controlled and many men chewed their tobacco instead. There was a match tub from which smokers could light their pipes and men were only allowed to smoke on the larboard side of the forecastle. Anyone caught smoking between sunset and sunrise was made to 'walk the gauntlet', which is to say, stripped to the waist and slowly passed between two lines of *garcette*-wielding men.

Officially, women were not allowed to stay on a ship overnight, even, according to the penal code, on public fête days. Officers would be held under arrest for a month and matelots put in irons if they ignored the rules. It must be remembered that, unlike their British foes, French sailors were allowed ashore and did have wives they could return to or prostitutes to visit in the port (see Plate B). The British were forced to allow prostitutes onto their ships in port because they were too scared of letting their pressed men ashore, affording them the opportunity to desert. The penal code made rape punishable with eight years in irons, rising to 12 years if violence or accomplices were involved and death if the woman was killed.

However, there is no doubt that women were on French ships, as two were plucked from the water at Trafalgar. Of the ladies in question one was named Jeannette and was with her husband onboard the *Achille*. During the battle she was stationed in the fore magazine and helped to pass cartridges up to the guns. When the ship caught fire, she went onto the gun deck and climbed out of a gun port, receiving burns from molten lead dripping from the deck above. Once in the sea she clung on to a plank of wood until rescued by the British and was later reunited with her husband. The other woman had also escaped the burning of the *Achille* by jumping in the sea and was forced to shed her clothing to prevent herself from drowning.

1 See Warrior 77: *French Soldier in Egypt*, Terry Crowdy and Christa Hook (Osprey Publishing, Oxford, 2003), for a description of this ceremony.

MEDICAL SERVICES

At a time when, by modern standards, medical practices were basic in the extreme, surgeons in the navy needed to be at the forefront of their profession if they were to have any chance of coping with the multitude of medical emergencies they might encounter at sea. In addition to combat and accidental injuries, sicknesses came in the form of seasickness, scurvy ('the most awful of maladies' according to Garneray), dysentery, typhus, typhoid, yellow fever and even bubonic plague in the Mediterranean. Therefore, in the medical schools at Brest, Rochefort and Toulon, a student naval doctor would be expected to learn physiological anatomy, surgical and medical pathology, naval hygiene, medical natural history, chemistry, practical pharmacy, clinical surgery, clinical medicine and midwifery.

Those that did fall sick during a voyage were kept in the hospice, a space between the main hatch and the stairs leading up to the ship's bell. The sailors who were assigned to scrubbing the decks had to wash this area every day, while the air was 'perfumed' twice daily, as directed by the chief medical officer, by burning pitch, vinegar or incense. The cots and blankets used by the sick were purified by gaseous hydrochloric acid, unless the patient had died of a pestilential sickness, in which case the cot and blanket were thrown into the sea.

If a man died, the ship's doctor would decide when the funeral would take place and notify the first-lieutenant. An interesting anecdote in Garneray's account regarding burials at sea, which always took place on the 'more honourable' starboard side of the vessel, recounts: 'At that time one used the cook's table to slide the corpses into the sea. Also, when a sailor wished the death of someone, he said that he would very much like to see them on the cook's table; it was a well used phrase then.'

To help tend to the sick, on each boat was a 'hospice master' in charge of the *cadres*, the wooden bed frames that could be hung by ropes from the ceiling or be placed on the deck as space permitted. He also maintained the canvas mattresses, blankets, sheets, greatcoats and cooking utensils embarked for the service of the sick. In addition to the hospice master, a number of matelots would serve as *fraters* or *infirmiers* (medical orderlies) during a voyage. The chief medical officer could grant these men a double ration of wine or brandy at busy times and recommend them for a gratification at the end of the voyage if they had shown particular compassion and humanity in their work.

The hospice master was charged with cooking for the sick. A regulation from 1784 set out the food to be given to the sick: this included tablets of bouillon, raisins, sorrel conserve (a traditional remedy for scurvy), pickled cabbage (sauerkraut), fresh bread, wine, raisins, honey or sugar. Dinner would be served at 11am comprising of soup, bread, wine and fresh meat. At 4pm supper would be served – prunes in sugar, rice and sugar, bread and wine.

With the cramped conditions accidents were commonplace. Garrison member Jacques-Louis Chieux remembered that

the heavy rolling of the ship uncoupled a 36 pound cannonball from its shot park, and it rolled against my right leg injuring me dangerously; it became gangrenous and I saw myself about to enter hospital. The gangrene increased more and more and I started to despair of my wound. The surgeon-major of the ship wanted to force me to enter Toulon hospital, which I never wanted to agree to, because I would be persuaded to lose the leg.

With amputation often the cure-all remedy of the day, Chieux's fear of hospitals was all too common. Fortunately, though, when his regiment was disembarked and quartered on the population outside Toulon he was offered an alternative to hospital treatment.

My hostess found me an old woman who helped to cure me with a regime of healthy living. I did not delay taking this choice, the gangrene decreased day by day and in less than a month the wound had become much better. This woman took all possible care of me, happy that I had not wanted to enter to the hospital 'for the butchers would have cut off the leg'.

Despite being more prevalent, accidental injuries and disease paled in comparison to the horrific injuries sustained in combat. Naval engagements were often fought at very close range – 'within pistol shot' was the description frequently given. When a cannonball struck the hull of a ship, not only would the ball penetrate through the wood, but it would also send up a shower of deadly splinters. While the cannonball would effortlessly cut a man in half, decapitate him, or amputate a limb, the splinters would cause equally severe wounds. In addition, close-quarter fighting would inflict deep lacerations, gunshot and puncture wounds.

The process of treating combat casualties was a production line of pain and horror. At the beginning of an action the surgeon would set up his equipment, normally consisting of forceps, knives, bone-saws and needles. Anaesthetic was unknown, but alcohol could be given, along with something to bite on; but in order to mute the inevitable barrage of screams and curses, the doctor's best hope was that his patient would pass out during the operation.

A wounded captain is carried below through thick clouds of gunpowder smoke. The wounded were kept on the *faux pont* (orlop deck) during combat and surgeons were forbidden from going above the waterline in action for fear of their being hit.

Men would be detailed to collect the injured and bring them down onto the orlop deck where they could be operated on. Casualties would be tended to by order of arrival and to add to the distress of those already wounded, they would be privy to the horrors taking place on the surgeon's table while waiting their turn. In the case of an amputation the patient was forcibly restrained while the doctor applied a tourniquet around the limb before using a knife to cut away the skin. A second, deeper incision would then go through the muscles and tendons. The surgeon would next saw through the bone then sew up the arteries and draw the loose skin over the stump. If the patient survived the shock of having a limb sawn off, there was a high probability of infection – only the very strong and fortunate would survive such an ordeal.

In addition to the more common wounds, Surgeon-Major Félix Charyau recorded several complicated combat injuries he attended:

> Aspirant Ruel had been struck on the right side of the head by a projectile which left a four inch wound that exposed part of the skull. He could only say one word ('thing') and used gestures to announce his desires. He recovered over a month and a half, but it was only with difficulty that he could pronounce another word.

A second case, suffering what would now be termed a psychological injury, involved an apprentice sailor: 'He had been at his post during the fighting, either through fright, or rather the loss of one of his close friends who was killed in action, he refused all food and died without the slightest sign of sickness.'

A more typical example of combat injury and the subsequent treatment received is given by Moreau de Jonnes. Struck by a splinter below the eye at the Battle of 1st June he recalled:

> When I went to find the surgeon to rid me of this tiresome visitor I was unpleasantly surprised to see him get out his knives, all bloody and splintered by the work to which he had been putting them, in order to open my face. I thanked him for his kind intentions but refused to accept his services.

Echoing Chieux's fear of hospitals, Moreau de Jonnes waited for dry land before seeking further medical help:

> On disembarking from the *Jemmapes* I had, in spite of my repugnance, to go to the Naval Hospital to be operated on. I presented myself to the chief surgeon, who was famous not only for his skill but for his eccentricity. There were some hundred people there awaiting his verdict and trembling for the safety of their persons. A young student obtained me a special pass on the pretext that I was a rare case. The learned man examined my damaged cheek and with a turn of the pincers succeed in extracting, comparatively painlessly, a long piece of wood which he exhibited in triumph to the spectators, who were astounded at his dexterity. 'You might have been blinded,' he remarked, and added, with the freedom of language which he usually affected: 'Don't worry, my lad. You will still be a mirror for some whores.'

A: Master gunner, 1798

B: Sailors of the Brest fleet, 1794

B

C: Sailors of the Brest fleet, 1794

c

D: At Trafalgar, 1805

E: At Trafalgar, 1805

E

F: At Trafalgar, 1805

G: At Trafalgar, 1805

G

The account goes on to explain how the hospital at Brest could not cope with the number of wounded cases after the battle. When cases of gangrene began to appear among the sick, de Jonnes was evacuated to another hospital:

> I left with a party for Pontanezen, a branch of the St. Louis hospital situated half a league outside Brest and usually reserved for convalescents. Everything was full, and we had to continue as far as Lesneven, a small town whose hospital was well reputed amongst sailors. On arrival I fainted, on coming to I became delirious, and for a week my condition was desperate. I had caught typhus. My youth, and above all the devoted care of Monsieur Despres, the house-doctor, saved my life. I owed much also to the Sisters of Charity, who treated me with true motherly care.

DISCIPLINE AND PUNISHMENT

In 1798 apprentice-helmsman Sanglé-Ferrière had his first taste of naval discipline when bound for Egypt. The expedition commander, Napoleon Bonaparte, told the assembled crew:

> The navy has been very neglected. One must re-establish the most severe discipline. I know there are a lot of novices in the fleet. It is for the officers to turn them into matelots. At the least fault, they will seize the *garcette*, and by employing it with vigour, make themselves obeyed.

Sanglé-Ferrière's reaction to this harangue was perhaps typical of many of his fellow novices: 'I became disenchanted and I realized that I had begun a career where thorns were more abundant than roses.'

Naval punishments had always been notoriously harsh. Although captains were in general paternalistic to their crews, when punishments were meted out, they were severe. Death sentences were carried out by firing squad or men were sentenced to the galleys, 'the living death'. *Galériens*, or *forçats* (convicts) as they were increasingly known, had originally been sentenced to a life at the oars of one of the king's fighting galleys. By the time of the Revolution, however, pairs of *galériens* were chained together and given hard labour in the ports.

Less serious offenders would find themselves flogged, forced to run the gauntlet, or sentenced to the *cale*. This punishment was a form of ducking, where the offender was seated on a handspike and plunged from the main yard into the sea below. It was known for a cannonball or two to be added to the handspike, aiding the victim's submersion, which would normally be repeated three times. However, the line was drawn at the *grand cale* (keel-hauling), which involved throwing the victim over one side of the boat and dragging him under the keel then up the other side. Victims would be torn to shreds by the shells of marine parasites attached to the hull and very often drowned. This punishment, apparently of Dutch origin, was seen as too inhumane to inflict on fellow Frenchmen. Equally, the *cale seche* (where the rope was cut short so the plunging victim would not reach the water at the end of the drop) was no longer practised.

In an evening session on 16 August 1790, the National Assembly heard the Navy Committee's report on punishment: '… the committee has examined the naval penal code; it has found it as lacking as it is rigorous: no graduation in punishment; an excessive severity; death or the galleys pronounced for crimes that human weakness excuses.' What the government decided to do, therefore, was introduce a whole host of lesser punishments to give the ship's captain an alternative to the severe punishments. This meant that where humanitarian captains may have once turned a blind eye to certain misdemeanours because of the severe penalty they would have to inflict, they could now pass a lesser sentence. As a sop to the crews, the accused men would have the right to be judged by their peers. A simple matelot would now be tried by a jury consisting of an officer, three officer-mariners and three fellow matelots. Unexpectedly for the government, this new penal code sparked a massive revolt in Brest. The 'lesser' punishments were considered humiliating: being tied to a mast or clapped in irons with a ball and chain was all too reminiscent of the treatment meted out to *galériens*.

The beginning of the 1790s was marked by a wave of disobedience, mutinies, officer resignations and general anarchy. In a spirit of revolution, crews saw fit to question and debate their orders, or in extreme cases to assassinate their officers. An interesting example of the trouble afflicting the navy at the beginning of 1793 was given by Athanase Postel, then serving as a ship's boy:

> I forgot to say that during our stay in Dunkirk harbour, as it was in the height of the Revolution, they made all the crew gather on the quarterdeck and made us sing Republican songs and cry '*Vive la République!*'. Every day they read the Penal Code to us as our heads were a little hot and, because it was forbidden to hit sailors, we always argued back. But we had an officer, Monsieur Gambart, from Dunkirk, who said, while speaking to a sailor who did not go

'Save yourselves, my friends, I shall stay at my post.' This engraving by Labrousse demonstrates the spirit the navy tried to instil through its penal code.

along with his ideas: 'I will not hit you, you bugger, but I will work you so hard, your heart will stop beating.'

However, once war was declared against Britain, the great maritime power of the age, the importance of having a disciplined navy suddenly dawned on the politicians in Paris. When the Toulon fleet was surrendered to the British and the Brest fleet disobeyed its orders in the Quiberon Bay mutiny, the government was forced into drastic action.

Towards the end of 1793 Jean-bon Saint-André, a member of the notorious *Comité de Salut Public*, went on a mission to Brest to forcibly reintroduce discipline among the crews and dock workers. The government's message was quite simple: further acts of mutiny would not be tolerated and naval discipline would be reinstated. Future transgressors would face the Revol̲_____'aris, followed by execution on the g_____ nal code was introduced on 10 Noven_____ -iment of trial by jury and reinforced th_____ enying sailors

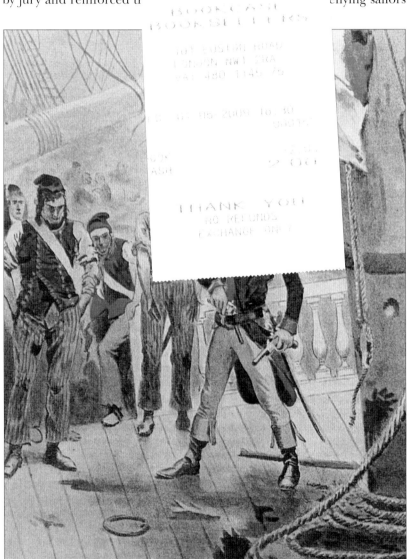

'Whoever talks about surrendering will be shot!' runs the caption of this lithograph by Le Blant. It is reported that during the Battle of 1st June one French ship fired at another that had struck its colours, forcing it to resume the fight.

the right to question or debate their orders. Although Saint-André's methods have since had many detractors, they appeared to work.

As first consul, Bonaparte also imposed a very strict code of discipline on the navy in 1801. As a sweetener, the regulation stated: 'It could be that these punishments might appear somewhat severe; but, in many circumstances, they are less than those pronounced by the majority of European maritime powers, all of which, like us, have recognized the need for exact discipline onboard ship.'

Punishments were divided into three classes. The least severe were 'disciplinary' punishments – ranging from the denial of wine rations or pay, to floggings, or being put in irons and incarcerated. The second type were 'afflictive' punishments such as running the gauntlet or being given the *cale*. The most severe sentence would remain death by firing squad.

The ship's captain would preside over a council of justice composed of the ship's *état-major*. In the most serious cases a council of war would be called, comprising a general officer of the fleet, three *capitaines de vaisseaux*, two *lieutenants de vaisseaux* and one *ensigne de vaisseau*, all aged over 30. In the event of a rebellion, or sedition in the face of the enemy, after consulting with his officers the ship's captain could order the death penalty on the spot.

Punishments were carried out in a manner to serve as a lesson to the whole crew. When a man was put in irons he was degraded in front of his shipmates and was declared incapable of serving on one of the state's ships. He was detained in the ship's hold until handed over to the port *gendarmes* and thrown into the nearest jail. When the death sentence was carried out, the ship would raise a red flag on its main mast and fire a single cannon shot. The crews of all the other ships in the fleet would be called up on deck and their captains would explain the reason for the sentence. The execution was by firing squad, with the victim shot in the back if guilty of treason or cowardice.

There are pages of offences listed in the regulations of which the following are just an example: When a boat signalled it was about to put to sea, anyone not on board within three hours was deducted a month's pay. Any man absent without permission for three consecutive days, or not rejoining the crew at the end of a period of leave, was posted as a deserter. If he subsequently came back voluntarily he would be locked in irons for the number of days he was absent and have his pay withheld; if he was arrested by force then he would be condemned to receive the *cale* and make a long-haul voyage as the lowest-ranking matelot. For a second offence, the deserter would be put in irons for five years.

For bringing unauthorized liquor or wine on board the offender would be fined three months' pay. A sailor absent from his watch would be deducted a month's pay while a guard at the powder magazine abandoning his post would be put in irons for four years. A man caught thieving from his crewmates would lose a month's pay and receive 12 lashes. Anyone hitting a comrade in a quarrel would be put in irons and then receive 12 lashes. Insubordination was punished with 12 lashes, or the *cale* if threats or gestures were used. The death sentence was applied for a number of offences, including espionage, treachery, unauthorized correspondence with the enemy, serving on an enemy ship, arousing revolt, bringing unauthorized flammable material (gunpowder, saltpetre, sulphur) onboard, lighting unauthorized fires, and pillage.

In order to strengthen the navy's resolve in battle, the penal code rigidly enforced tactical doctrine. Both Saint-André and later Napoleon made sure that their ships' captains feared failing their missions as much as facing the enemy. The code declared that anyone not engaging an enemy of inferior or equal strength without good reason would be cashiered. The death sentence was applied to all captains who struck their colours, except in the following circumstances: after being boarded and captured; if a fire on the ship was out of control; if the ship was sinking and the pumps were unable to cope; after having the major masts or rudder shot off; or after having completely run out of ammunition. If a ship was hopelessly outnumbered and a council of war ratified the decision, a captain could strike without meeting the other criteria. Any officer who ordered the colours struck, other than the commander of the ship, or any crewman that carried it out, was to be punished with death. In the event of surrender, the commander was to save his crew and throw away all sensitive papers before trying to burn or hole the ship rather than allowing it to be taken as a prize. Under pain of death, the captain was to be the last to leave the ship.

THE EXPERIENCE OF BATTLE

The intense concentration of firepower in major fleet actions dwarfed anything seen in the land battles of the age. As an example, compare General Marmont's decisive 'massed battery' of 18 small-calibre field guns at Marengo against the broadsides of a single 74-gun battleship. For sheer destructive power, even Napoleon's famous 80-gun battery at Waterloo in 1815 pales into insignificance when compared with the artillery used at Trafalgar ten years before. Gicquel remembered an amusing anecdote clearly illustrating the effect of naval artillery on newcomers to combat at sea:

> Near to him [the ship's captain] was found a brave infantry colonel who had proved himself at Marengo, but whom the volley from the *Temeraire* troubled profoundly. He looked vainly to shelter behind the powerful stature of our captain, who, on seeing this, said: 'Look, Colonel, do you think I am plated in copper?' We could not help ourselves but laugh despite the gravity of the moment.

The accounts left by survivors of naval engagements leave us with no doubt that they were traumatic, exhausting episodes. Many were left with a sense of awe by what they had witnessed, as attested in the following piece by Moreau de Jonnes:

> When I went on deck the following morning I was literally astounded by the magnificent spectacle offered by the two fleets sailing on the same course, as though in concert, and almost abreast of one another. One saw there sixty line-of-battle ships in line ahead with colours flying and the guns showing through the open ports, accompanied by as many frigates and a swarm of brigs and dispatch boats … The two fleets kept on the same tack for a

Close-quarter naval warfare descended into a trial of strength and willpower. On the eve of battle, to ensure his crew was in the best possible shape before Trafalgar, Captain Lucas on the *Redoutable* remembered 'as I was certain of there being an engagement the next day, and I made most of the officers and crew go to bed to have them in good condition.'

long while; they then approached one another and were soon within gunshot. We could see the open battery ports and the gaping muzzles of the guns. We saw the riflemen in the tops ready to pick off the officers or the Admiral on his quarterdeck. Great nets were spread above the deck to protect the men from falling blocks and tackle.

In fleet actions the French relied on the tactic of holding their ships in a defensive line, which allowed them to concentrate their broadsides on approaching enemy vessels and protected the vulnerable sterns of their own ships. The rear of a ship, where the captain's quarters were located, was only lightly protected. If a ship was able to place itself across the stern of another (to *passé en poupe*), its cannonballs could travel through the entire length of the opposing ship, dismounting guns from their carriages and killing large numbers of crewmen. Paramount importance, therefore, was given to holding a tight line, so much so that Saint-André declared that any officer allowing the line to be broken in front of his ship would be guillotined. If a gap opened in the line due to a damaged ship lagging behind for any reason, all the ships behind would

Ships marked with an asterisk were captured, *Le Vengeur* was sunk in action. Not shown is *Le Tyrannicide* (74), which was out of the line during the battle.

VII. FRENCH ORDER OF BATTLE 1ST JUNE 1794

SHIPS OF THE LINE		FRIGATES	
La Convention (74)	Le Jacobin (80)	La Proserpine	La Gentile
Le Gasparin (74)	Achille (74)*	La Surprise	La Felictié
L'Amerique (74)*	Le Patriote (74)	L'Insurgente	La Bellone
Le Terrible (110)	Le Vengeur (74)	La Résolue	La Précieusse
L'Impétueux (74)*	Le Northumberland (74)*	La Nayade	La Tamise
L'Eole (74)	Le Jemappes (80)	La Galathée	La Semillante
Le Mucius (74)	L'Entreprenant (74)		
Le Touville (74)	Neptune (74)	**CORVETTES**	
Le Trajan (74)	Le Républicain (118)	Le Maireguiton	L'Atalante
Le Trente-un Mai (74)	Le Sanspareil (80)*	Le Furet	La Mouche
L'Audacieux (74)	Scipion (80)	La Mutine	Le Papillon
Le Juste (80)*	Le Mont-blanc (74)	Le Jean Bart	Le Courier
La Montagne (120)	Le Pelletier (74)		

VIII. BATTLE OF THE NILE 1798

Le Guerrier (74)	*taken* (1)
Le Conquerant (74)	*taken*
Le Spartiate (74)	*taken*
L'Aquilon (74)	*taken*
Le Peuple Souverain (74)	*taken*
Le Franklin (80)	*taken*
L'Orient (120)	*burnt*
Le Tonnant (80)	*taken*
Le Heureux (74)	*taken* (1)
Le Timoleon (74)	*burnt*
Le Guillaume Tell (80)	*escaped*
Le Mercure (74)	*taken* (1)
Le Généreux (74)	*escaped*

Those ships marked with a (1) were later burnt as unserviceable. In addition to these ships, the frigate *La Sérieuse* was sunk and *L'Artemis* burnt.

have to increase speed to close the gap. In the event of an enemy ship trying to break the line, Saint-André said the captains should prefer to be boarded rather than allow the oncoming ship to break through.

Against the British, French crews experienced considerable technical and tactical disadvantages when it came to gunnery. French crews were taught to fire at the masts of enemy ships rather than their hulls. Wooden ships were rarely sunk by artillery fire, but if an enemy ship could be crippled through being dismasted then there was more chance of avoiding pursuit or taking it as a prize. Gicquel explained that there were problems with this tactic:

We had then the principle of firing at the masts, but to produce significant damage there, we lost a mass of projectiles, which aimed at the hull of the enemy ship would have knocked out part of its crew. Our losses were always incomparably higher than those of the English, who fired horizontally and struck us full-on, sending splinters flying that were much more murderous than the projectile itself.

To target the masts of an enemy ship it was necessary to fire on the upward roll of the ship, thus giving the guns greater elevation. Achieving an accurate shot depended on there being very little delay between the ignition of the priming charge and the subsequent ignition of the main charge in the barrel. Gicquel admitted that: 'We were still using linstock, which ignited the charge with a despairing slowness, so that if the ship rolled a lot, which was the case on 21 October [1805, at Trafalgar], entire broadsides passed above the masts without causing them least damage.'

For ships attempting to maintain a strict line of battle, the vast clouds of gunpowder smoke soon severed all means of communication between vessels, prompting the French to use the smaller frigates to take messages around the fleet. Moreau de Jonnes gave a vivid description of the eerie blanket of smoke enveloping his ship:

Instead of a uniform grey colour it varied not only in tint but in intensity according to the circumstances. Sometimes it was a thick sooty black, gleaming with sparks and suddenly stabbed with ruddy flame; then again it was transparent, giving to the light of day the appearance of moonlight and blotting out objects by a fantastic sort of mirage. It was frequently sown with brownish circles floating upwards horizontally, which recalled those traced by medieval painters above the heads of saints … When the cloud split, some enemy ship, girdled with its double or triple band of red or yellow, loomed up, her side bristling with guns ready to crush us with their thunder. Soon this floating fortress, gathering the feeble breeze in its immense spread of canvas, came nearer and seemed to cover itself in flame. An appalling explosion was heard and a hail of enormous cannon shot crashed through the wooden walls which served us for a parapet. Often we forestalled this murderous discharge by that of all our guns and when, through the smoke wreaths, we could see that we had brought down a mast or a yard, or stove in a bulwark and made a large breach in the enemy's battery, then a cry of triumph arose which raised the courage of our companions less favoured by the fortune of war.

While the gun crews and infantry maintained their fire, artificers would be busy clearing damage, cutting away fallen timbers and plugging holes. In one action Garneray watched as British sailors tried to make running repairs to battle damage:

> These unfortunates, lowering themselves over the side by ropes, tried to nail down some planks, or hammer in wooden plugs, mattresses and heaps of oakum. But alas! Each of these hardy workers suffered a hideous death. Some, crushed, literally speaking, by our cannonballs, covered the side of the ship with hideous and bloody debris. The others, mortally wounded, fell and disappeared suddenly, sinking in the foam thrown up by our cannonballs. Others, more unfortunate still, also hit by our iron, seized a rope and were dragged along in the wake of the ship which they turned crimson with their blood, shouting heartbreaking cries of distress and calling for help. Their shrill cries cut through the resonant noise of the cannon and reached us, but we remained insensible. In fact, we especially directed our fire on those that came to save them.

Perhaps the biggest problems came when one or more of the ship's masts came down as a result of enemy fire. On board the *Bucentaure* at Trafalgar, the purser's log recorded:

> The mizzen mast fell first, followed by the main mast and both to the starboard side. In falling they knocked down the lids to the gun ports and prevented the batteries coming into play. Vainly we tried to disencumber them, but the enemy canister fire swept the deck in a horrible manner and we were obliged to give up.

Similar problems were encountered by Moreau de Jonnes at the Battle of 1st June:

> Whilst we were replying to a seventy-four, a second came to attack us on our other side. We were pounded by them for more than an

Those marked with a (1) arrived in Cadiz but were unserviceable; those marked (2) were subsequently captured on 2 November. Combined with 15 Spanish ships, the combined fleet had a total of 2,648 guns.

IX. FATE OF FRENCH SHIPS AT TRAFALGAR 1805			
Bucentaure (80)	lost	Aigle (74)	lost
Formidable (80)	escaped (2)	Scipion (74)	escaped (2)
Neptune (80)	escaped	Duguay-Trouin (74)	escaped (2)
Indomptable (80)	lost	Berwick (74)	lost
Algésiras (74)	escaped (1)	Argonaute (74)	escaped (2)
Pluton (74)	escaped (1)	Achille (74)	burned
Mont-Blanc (74)	escaped (2)	Redoutable (74)	lost
Intrépide (74)	lost	Fougueux (74)	lost
Swiftsure (74)	captured	Héros (74)	escaped

hour. Our foremast was shot away close to the deck; the mainmast broke in half, and the fall of one brought down the other. The shock was so violent that in the lower battery we all thought the ship was splitting in two. As a matter of fact our situation was little better. The masts with their yards, sails, and tackle hung alongside, half in the water, and weighing on the ship gave her such a list that she seemed about to turn turtle. We all ran to close the ports. It was high time; the water was already coming into the lower batteries and we were going under. The crew, headed by the most active among the officers, armed themselves with sharp axes and set about cutting away all shrouds and rigging which attached the wrecked masts to the ship.

As *L'Intrépide* closed nearer to the English ships at Trafalgar, crewmen began to think of boarding an enemy ship. As the ship

In battle the 'tops' on the masts soon became redoubts from where musketry and grenades would rain down on an enemy ship. Notice the boarding axe hooked on the belt of the figure loading to the left.

entered the fray the *aspirant* Gicquel took up his combat station. 'I spent the whole time in combat on the forecastle where I was charged with manoeuvre and the musketry; it was also from there that I could lead any boarding company, it was my most ardent desire which I could unfortunately never realize.'

With an intense rivalry dating back centuries, Garneray describes the bitterness of the struggle between French and British sailors when meeting in combat:

> On both sides, the matelots, armed to the teeth, distributed in the rigging, hanging from all sides of the ship, waiting, eyes ablaze, mouthing insults, cheeks purple with rage, for the moment to board … Not only did the fusillade continue ardent and sharp, at point blank, but there were matelots who, not finding enough satisfaction for their hatred in squeezing their finger on the trigger of their weapon, threw down their muskets on the deck and seized anything more murderous that came to their hands, throwing them at the enemy, accompanied by damnations unknown until that day.

With communication lost and falling masts preventing manoeuvre, the engagement would often become pell-mell with opposing ships crashing against each other and inflicting point-blank devastation with their broadsides. At Trafalgar, Robert Guillemard on the *Redoutable* recalled the moment when his dismasted ship was put between the fire of the *Victory* and the *Temeraire*, with a second French ship then attacking *Victory*:

> The rigging was abandoned, and every sailor and soldier put to the guns; the officers themselves had nothing to provide for, nothing to order in this horrible conflict and came likewise to the guns. Amidst nearly four hundred pieces of heavy cannon all firing at one time in a confined space – amidst the noise of the balls, which made furious breaches in the sides of the *Redoutable* – amongst the splinters which flew in every direction with the speed of projectiles, and the dashing of the vessels, which were driven by the waves against each other, not a soul thought of anything but destroying the enemy, and the cries of the wounded and the dying were no longer heard. The men fell, and if they were any impediment to the action of the gun they had just been working, one of their companions pushed them aside with his foot to the middle of the deck, and without uttering a word, placed himself with concentrated fury at the same post, where he soon experienced a similar fate.

Hellish scenes below decks were also experienced by Garneray:

> During the two hours that the cannonade lasted, our men's zeal and ardour was admirable: blinded by smoke, overwhelmed by the burning heat, they had thrown off their clothes and resembled demons dancing in a furnace. The majority, having slipped on the lifeless corpses of their comrades in the batteries, were completely covered in blood: it was horrible to have seen.

Garneray then went on to explain the necessity of removing the dead as quickly as possible: 'As for the corpses, which obstructed circulation and blocked the manoeuvre, we threw them quickly and without ceremony over the side, without regret, attention, or farewell following them to the seabed. Who knows if, among them, there were not some whose hearts still beat!'

For the crews of crippled ships, the *coup de grace* would be administered if an enemy ship broke through the line and passed behind the stern, or to use the British expression, crossed the 'T'. Again, Moreau de Jonnes leaves us with no doubt about the effects of such a move:

> Without sails or the means to use them we were nailed to the spot unable to defend ourselves. Realizing our desperate situation a three-decker placed herself across our stern … It was really equivalent to hitting a man when he was down, murdering the wounded and mutilating the dead. In the position in which we were none of our guns would bear, and we had no alternative but to allow ourselves to be shot to bits without resistance. It is true that the shortness of the range prevented the enemy from using all his guns, but half of them sufficed to produce an appalling slaughter and sink the *Jemmapes* under our feet. In fact, the first discharge from his three batteries swept our decks, dismounted our heavy guns, and sent shot down into the hold where they finished off our wounded. Our loss would have been even greater had not our officers ordered the gunners to lie flat when they saw the English take up their portfires.

Caught by a larger vessel in a separate battle, Garneray's ship took a fearful battering and began to tilt to starboard.

> A moment of confusion and indescribable stupor followed: only with great difficulty did our men escape from the water that

overran their posts and take refuge on the port side: our gun decks were submerged, our decks exposed. The English did not lessen their fire. After this misfortune without remedy, which neither intrepidity nor skill could have surmounted, all resistance became impossible: all that was left was, like Roman gladiators, to die with dignity … The spectacle presented was as sad as it was terrible. The rails were almost levelled; the deck, ploughed by cannonballs, was littered with hideously disfigured corpses and bloody human debris.

Onboard the *Redoutable* at Trafalgar, Guillemard witnessed similar scenes of devastation:

The mutilated bodies of our companions encumbered the two decks, which were covered with shot, broken cannon, matches still smoking, and shattered timbers. One of our thirty-six pounders had burst towards the close of the contest. The thirteen men placed at it had been killed by the splinters, and were heaped together round its broken carriage. The ladders that led between the different decks were shattered and destroyed; the mizzen-mast and main-mast had fallen, and encumbered the deck with blocks and pieces of rigging.

Moreau de Jonnes remembered:

I was filled with a sense of horror which no amount of reasoning could conquer, at the aspect of the charnel-house which once had been the lower battery. To start with it had been necessary to put the wounded there, for whom there was no room in the hospital on the orlop deck; then, when the orlop deck had to be abandoned owing to the water, we had to haul up these wretched

At such close proximity, the hull of a ship would offer scant protection to the crew within. Many considered the wooden splinters thrown out by an impact far more dangerous than the ball itself.

creatures, mostly dangerously or even mortally wounded, and put them side by side in two lines in the battery.

Jacques-Louis Chieux, an infantryman in *16e de ligne*, saw action at Trafalgar on board the *Intrépide*. After two hours of fighting several British ships, with the hold taking in water and its masts shot away and around a third of the crew casualties, the *Intrépide* struck its colours and was boarded by a prize crew of several English officers and 50 Marines and sailors. Chieux described the measures taken to repair the ship:

> The gunners made fast the cannons, others washed the beams, the carpenters, caulkers and sail makers blocked the holes that the cannonballs had made, while soldiers and sailors manned the pumps and drew the water from the hold … Those who were sick and wounded were most at pity.

Worse horror was to come to some unfortunate crews, for more than sinking, sailors feared fire breaking out onboard. One of the most

Detail of a typical boarding action from the period. French crews preferred to use pikes to repel boarders.

infamous moments of the Napoleonic Wars at sea came in 1798 with the explosion onboard the flagship *l'Orient* at the Battle of the Nile. In recent years marine archaeologists have revealed that the ship suffered two simultaneous and gigantic explosions, probably caused by the ignition of gunpowder stores at either end of the hold. The explosion itself was so strong that the ship's massive rudder was catapulted over half a mile with the sound being heard 20 miles away in Rosetta.

Robert Guillemard reported the fate of another French ship that burned, this time at Trafalgar:

> The *Achille*, in which was a detachment of the 67th regiment, was set on fire during the action, The English who were fighting it

In smaller engagements boarding operations were carried out by sending troops on the ship's boats. Charles Dunand serving with the corsair captain Pollet gives a graphic example of how close-order weapons were used to repel these attacks: 'The Captain seized a dozen loaded and cocked pistols in his left arm; sitting astride the bulwarks, with one foot on the quarterdeck and the other on the poop of the English longboat, he was the centre of a hurricane of swords. As he fired each pistol he hurled it at the head of the English. Lescot brought down an Englishman with each of his shots, and with a boarding axe I cut off the wrists of those who were trying to clamber on board. Occasionally I struck an English head.'

cleared off; and of eight hundred men, who formed the crew, not more than twenty found an opportunity of escaping. When all hopes of stopping the progress of the flames were gone, and death seemed inevitable, to avoid waiting for it several officers blew out their brains; others threw themselves into the flames that were consuming the forepart of the ship; several sailors went to the store-room, gorged themselves with brandy, and, by the most complete drunkenness, endeavoured to throw a veil over the disaster that was about to terminate their existence. Towards six o'clock in the evening the fire reached the gun-room, the vessel blew up, and everything disappeared.

AFTER THE BATTLE

'Heavens, what a sad situation and a painful moment for those unfortunates who were drowning and for those who were floating and calling for help! But all feelings of humanity seemed to have died.'

This poignant description of the aftermath of Trafalgar was made by *Cannonier* Guillain and is perhaps typical of the feeling of many survivors of large naval engagements. The survivors were faced with a disaster they were hardly equipped to manage. As night drew a veil over his first battle, Moreau de Jonnes remembered: 'Nothing was heard except the sound of the pumps and the hammers of the caulkers, who struggled to prevent the sea from swallowing both conqueror and conquered and distributing them impartially to the sharks.'

His ordeal continued into the morning:

I remember the following morning hearing a lot of splashing alongside and asking a quartermaster the reason of it. 'It's *Père* Simon,' he replied, 'a shipmate of thirty years standing; we have just thrown him overboard, and the sharks are fighting over his body.' These terrible creatures swam alongside in veritable flocks waiting for the bodies to be thrown over … Without being actually wounded I was little better off; my limbs and body were covered with painful bruises and bleeding scratches. The detonation of the thirty-six pounders a few inches from my ears had made me deaf, and my arms were practically dislocated by the enormous weight of the heavy calibre sponge and rammer which I had had to manipulate during the battle.

Damaged ships that had avoided capture now had to limp home to port either on tow or under the jury-rigged masts. However, surviving battle was no guarantee of reaching home again safely. After Trafalgar the *Indomitable* reached the entrance to Cadiz harbour with 1,500 men on board, including

Excerpt from Pierre Chas' contemporary patriotic ode relating the 'sublime devotion' shown by the *Vengeur*'s crew who refused to surrender while sinking at the Battle of 1st June.

> The English thunder combines
> Uniting against *Le Vengeur*,
> Whose sides were half open, the sails torn,
> Soon offering nothing but a spectacle of horror.
> But these dying warriors of noble courage,
> Brave all the dangers, face up to their sinking,
> Knowing to preserve their greatness until the end
> And to meet to their destiny;
> The glory of this day
> Refusing to live at the expense of their honour.
>
> Suddenly the tumult ceases,
> And calm succeeds the shouts of the pain;
> The flag rises,
> Displaying its triple colours.
> *Vive la liberté*! *Vive la République*!
> Such are the last shouts of these generous hearts,
> For whom the most awful moment,
> Is no more than a civic fete.
>
> Give to the Homeland a new example,
> The sea, they say, provides us with a tomb.
> Lo, the ocean's deep abyss,
> Before the eyes of an astonished enemy,
> Receives these illustrious victims,
> And swallows *Le Vengeur's* remains

some from the flagship *Bucentaure*. However, before it could reach safety, it fell victim to what was known as the 'fortunes of the sea'. A storm broke and the heavily battle-damaged ship was split in two on the coast. *Cannonier* Guillain recorded the story told by the survivors:

> Fourteen hundred men were taking refuge on the prow of the vessel; they held on to one another and beseeched the heavens to bring them help. Several of the wounded, of which the boat was full, were pulled onto the poop deck; they raised their hands to the sky and implored the assistance of God who alone could save them at this fatal moment. All their prayers were in vain. The sea broke with rage and the hull, which had been worn out in the fighting, could no longer resist the storm. Two hundred men only reached the shore, some, seeing themselves about to be crushed by the debris of the ship, swam to safety, the others, tossed by the force of the sea, were thrown onto the sand.

Life in captivity

For many French sailors and soldiers at sea, an indefinite spell of captivity in Britain was a very real prospect. Between 1803 and 1814 well over 120,000 POWs were sent to Britain, approximately two-thirds of whom were sailors. In the same period only 17,000 were exchanged for British prisoners in French hands, while another 10,000 died from sickness. Some managed to escape and others were sent home because

Review by a naval prefect. Under the Imperial era, sailors were militarized and more strictly regulated. Later in the period many served as infantry on land.

of illness or infirmity, but for the vast majority, the greater part of the Napoleonic Wars was spent in prison depots like Porchester, Perth, Plymouth, Dartmoor and Norman Cross, or on prison ships, the infamous hulks anchored at Chatham or Portsmouth.

Captive officers enjoyed much greater freedom, being distributed across the country to provincial 'parole towns' where they could live among the local population with a certain amount of freedom, comfort and, in many cases, a degree of celebrity. Officers were normally confined to within one mile in any direction from the town centre and if on the ringing of a bell each evening they were not in their quarters or their whereabouts was otherwise unknown they would be fined. In addition, many French officers were Freemasons and received aid from British masons or formed their own lodges, 'The Sons of Mars and Neptune' being a popular lodge name among prisoners.

At the end of the Revolutionary period in 1800 there had been 22,000 French POWs held in Britain. In previous wars French governments had

Admiral Eustache Bruix (1759–1805), shown as a Grand Admiral of the Republic and commander of the flotilla against Britain. A former *Garde de la Marine*, Bruix was promoted *capitaine de vaisseau* in 1793. After a short period in the wilderness as a noble, Bruix took command of the *Indomitable*, then the *Eole*, before being made *contre-amiral* (rear admiral) in 1797. After serving as the Naval and Colonial Minister (1798–1799) Bruix retired due to health reasons, returning to command the Boulogne Flotilla from 15 July 1803.

supplied clothing and paid a small penny-a-day allowance to its men held prisoner. However, on coming to power Napoleon refused to send clothing to the prisoners, decreeing that it was the captive power's responsibility to supply them. When conditions among the prisoners deteriorated and many began to die, France accused Britain of inhumanity. British officials pointed out that the rations were adequate, although Frenchmen would have preferred a greater amount of bread against what was to them an increased meat ration. Officials admitted that some captives were indeed reduced to a semi-naked state, but only because they had gambled away their clothes or bartered them for tobacco. With the plight of prisoners causing just concern, in the winter of 1800/1801 the British government felt compelled to supply them with new clothes.

Although captivity could never be described as a welcome state of affairs, it is wrong to believe that the prisoners' plight was uniformly miserable. Within the walls of their prisons some captives became successful traders, setting up markets to sell provisions including tobacco, beer and fresh vegetables to supplement official rations. These markets were supplied from outside the prisons by locals who were monitored to ensure they traded at the normal market price. To purchase goods at these markets, many prisoners received money from home as it was permitted to send letters back and forth across the Channel. Letters from French prisoners in England usually went to Plymouth or Dover and were sent to France by a vessel sailing under a flag of truce, usually entering France via Morlaix or Calais.

In addition to money sent from home, the prisoners were quite free to sell anything they manufactured and with the diversity of tradesmen among captured sailors, considerable sums of money were there to be made. Even on the prison hulks, life could be made tolerable with a little enterprise. A prisoner from Trafalgar held on a hulk at Chatham, Jacques-Louis Chieux, explained that within six months of captivity:

> … The masters of writing, arithmetic, of arms and of dance used their talents and made many good pupils. The cobblers and tailors set up their boutiques. The soldiers and sailors with no trade amused themselves making small ships from bone, dice, dominoes, etc. … The cobblers and tailors were without cease occupied by the bourgeois of Chatham and around, the others sold their merchandises as soon as it was manufactured. There were some prisoners that did not work, who did the chores for those that were occupied and would by this means earn enough to maintain themselves. At the end of 7 or 8 months of captivity, the interior of the hulk was unrecognizable, all the gun ports

Denis Decrès (1761–1820), lithography by Lanvin. Decrès was Napoleon's naval minister from 1801 to 1814 and also during the Hundred Days in 1815. A *Garde de la Marine* in 1779, the Revolution found Decrès on service abroad. Returning to France in 1794, he was dismissed for being a noble, then reintegrated in 1795. Promoted *contre-amiral* (rear admiral) in 1798, he was chosen by Napoleon to command the frigates on the Egyptian expedition. Maritime Prefect of Lorient in 1800, he was called to the naval ministry. An advocate of war against commerce, he championed the cause of frigate building after defeat at Trafalgar.

were glazed, everyone was occupied with their work and the gun deck presented a curious sight to foreigners who came to see us.

BIBLIOGRAPHY

Jean Boudriot's monumental multi-volume study on the French *Vaisseau de 74* is an absolute necessity to anyone interested in ship design and the French Navy at the end of the *ancien régime*. His fourth volume is filled with the minutiae on the handling of the ship, its armaments and crew. The British Library has a copy of Lescallier's invaluable 1798 illustrated naval vocabulary in addition to some of his other works. Artefacts can be seen in the Musée de la Marine in Paris (www.musee-marine.fr) and also in the Royal Maritime Museum at Greenwich (www.nmm.ac.uk). Progress on salvage operation in Egypt of the remains of the 118-gun *L'Orient* can be accessed at www.franckgoddio.com. The mammoth *Recueil des lois relatives a la marine et aux colonies*, government archives and other contemporary documents can be sourced online at www.gallica.bnf. In addition to these resources the following works have been consulted:

Boudriot, Jean (trans. by David H. Roberts). *The seventy-four gun ship*, 4 Vols (Paris: Jean Boudriot, 1986–1988)

Cormack, William S. *Revolution & Political Conflict in the French Navy 1789–1794* (Cambridge: Cambridge University Press, 1995)

Depeyre, Michel. *Tactiques et Stratégies Navales de la France et du Royaume-Uni de 1690 à 1815* (Paris: Economica, 1998)

Foreman, Laura, & Ellen Blue Phillips. *Napoleon's Lost Fleet* (London: Discovery Books, 1999)

Fraser, Edward. *The Enemy at Trafalgar* (London: Hodder & Stoughton, 1906)

Garneray, A. L. *Voyages, Aventures et Combats. Souvenirs de ma vie maritime* (Paris: 1851)

Guillemard, Robert. *The Adventures of a French Sergeant* (London: Hutchinson & Co., 1898)

Jonnes, Alexandre Moreau de. *Aventures de Geurre au temps de la République et du Consulat*, 2 Vols (Paris: 1858). See also trans. by Cyril Hammond *Adventures In The Revolution And Under The Consulate* (London: Peter Davis Limited, 1929)

Lescallier, Daniel Baron. *Vocabulaire des termes de marine anglois et françois* (Paris: 1798)

Postel, Athanase. *Mémoires d'un Corsair et Aventurier* (Rennes: La Découvrance, 2001)

Stark, Suzanne J. *Female Tars – women aboard ship in the age of sail* (London: Constable, 1996)

Teissedre F. (ed). *Souvenirs, Journal et Correspondance sur l'Expédition d'Égypte et l'Armée d'Orient* (Paris: Librairie Historique Teissedre F., 1998)

Teissedre F. (ed). *Souvenirs de marins du Premier Empire* (Paris: Librairie Historique Teissedre F., 1998)

Teissedre F. (ed). *La marine et les colonies sous le premier Empire. Journaux et Souvenirs* (Paris: Librairie Historique Teissedre F., 2000)

Teissedre F. (ed). *Trafalgar et la marine du Premier Empire* (Paris: Librairie Historique Teissedre F., 2001)

COLOUR PLATE COMMENTARY

A: MASTER GUNNER, 1798

This Marine artillery sergeant-major doubles as the master gunner on his ship. From 1795 the uniform of the Marine artillery regiments (*demi-brigades* before 1803) included a blue *habit* (coat) and *veste* (under-jacket), bordered in scarlet with a red collar and cuff flap on the sleeve. The breeches were blue, the buttons yellow with an anchor surrounded by the legend 'Republic Française' (Napoleon added two crossed cannons to the anchor motif and replaced the legend with the regimental title). The *chapeau* (hat) was bordered with a black woollen stripe and decorated with a red pompon; the tricolour cockade was held in place with a yellow woollen strip attached by a small uniform button. In addition, corporals and gunners received a blue *paletot* (sailor's jacket) and a pair of cloth trousers for heavy work and fatigues in port as well as for training in. The equipment belts were black leather (white after 1803) and the short sabre was only worn by NCOs and first-class gunners. Napoleon stipulated that each gunner was provided with *petit équipement* consisting of a hide haversack, three shirts, three handkerchiefs, a pair of black gaiters, a pair of grey short canvas gaiters, two pairs of shirts, three pairs of stockings, two collars, a bag of hair powder, brushes, a comb, shoe buckles, *queue* (pigtail) ribbon, vent-pick and hat pompon. Once assigned to a vessel, the troops would receive two blue shirts, a *paletot*, a pair of canvas overalls, a hammock and a blanket, along with the requisite number of *bidons*, *gamelles* and other utensils for their messes. Also shown is artillery equipment including (1) a sponge, (2) a worm, for extracting debris from the barrel, and (3) a rammer. He is holding a *faneau de combat* (lit. battle lantern) with polished bone lenses rather than glass, hung to provide light for the gun crews at night.

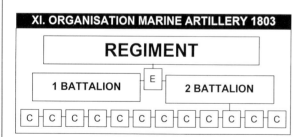

XI. ORGANISATION MARINE ARTILLERY 1803

REGIMENT

1 BATTALION — E — 2 BATTALION

C C C C C C C C C C C

The six regiments were each composed of an *état-major* (E) and two battalions, each with ten companies (C). The *état-majors* would include one *chef de brigade*, two battalion commanders, two adjudant-majors, one quartermaster-treasurer, one medical officer, two adjudant NCOs, one drum-major, one drum-corporal, one master-tailor, one master-cobbler, one master-armourer and eight musicians including a leader. In peacetime, each company would include three officers and 80 men, including: one captain, one first-lieutenant, one second-lieutenant, one sergeant-major, four sergeants, one *caporal-fourrier*, eight corporals, 16 gunners (*cannoniers*) 1st class, 16 gunners 2nd class, 32 *canonniers aspirants* and two drummers. In wartime an additional 32 *cannonniers aspirants* would be added to each company.

B AND C: SAILORS OF THE BREST FLEET, 1794

Breton sailors enjoy one last night on land before setting out to meet the British Channel fleet at the Battle of 1st June. A rather young and naive Moreau de Jonnes gives a wonderful description of these last hours before the departure of the fleet:

> At the sound of the port's bell which announced the cessation of work, some twelve to fifteen thousand men dashed through the gates like escaped schoolboys. They wished to enjoy their freedom and profit by their existence while they were sure of it, for

The gateway to the arsenal of Brest. Gicquel was in the port at the same time as de Jonnes in 1794 and was unimpressed: 'Licentiousness was everywhere. With the real sailors captive or embarked, it had been necessary to engage men from the dregs of society, for the majority had been involved in the most dreadful massacres, and were happy to escape from the condemnation of their fellow-citizens. They were from Brest, Nantes and all over, and it was the most appalling collection of bandits. These people did everything possible to remain on land, and I experienced a true relief when I was registered on the crew roles of the frigate the *Gentille*.'

Portrait of a *capitaine de vaisseau*, presumed to be Jérôme Bonaparte (1784–1860), showing the detail of the 1804 coat with embroidered anchors (nine each side and two on the scarlet collar). Napoleon's younger brother began his naval career as an *aspirant* in 1801 and had risen to the rank of *Capitaine de Vaisseau* by September 1805. It is fair to assume that this meteoric rise was not directly a result of any particular talent as a mariner.

was hoisted in an imposing manner, the fifers and drummers beating *au drapeau*, the musketeers presenting arms … The enemy column directing itself on our battle line came into range. The *Bucentaure* and its forward escort opened fire. I was on the quarterdeck with a number of my gun commanders. I remarked to them how our ships were firing poorly, as all their shots were falling too low. I advised them to fire to de-mast and above all to aim well. At 11.45 the *Redoutable* opened fire with a shot from Number 1 Battery which cut the yard off the *Victory*'s fore-topsail, as it steered towards the *Redoutable*'s foremast. Cries of joy resounded in all the batteries. Our fire was well fed: in less than ten minutes, the same vessel had lost its mizzen mast, its small top mast and its main mast's topgallant sail … The damage to the *Victory* did nothing to change Admiral Nelson's audacious manoeuvre: he still persisted in wanting to cut the line in front of the *Redoutable* and threatened to ram us if we opposed them. The close proximity of this vessel, followed by the *Temeraire*, far from intimidating our crew, did nothing but augment its courage; and to prove to the English admiral that we did not fear being boarded, I ordered the grappling hooks to be hoisted up onto

there only remained 24 hours before having the ocean beneath their feet, a furious tempest over their heads and a triple battery of English guns loaded with canister in front of them. This near and threatening destiny did not affect their cheerfulness, on the contrary it excited them and I have never seen people so joyous since then … In the blink of an eye, the city became an enormous pothouse, where each amused himself in his own way. The Recouvrance district became a vast cabaret; a certain street in the old town, that of the *Sept-Saints* was lined with thousands of drinkers sitting at tables along its whole length; the houses could not contain them. Outside the gates, the pleasures were more varied and less innocent: there were balls where the dancers resembled Athenian courtesans, at the fixed price of three oboles. For a long time I believed they were the most horrid women in the universe and I was only proved wrong when I saw those of Portsmouth. One day, three cannon shots were heard. The bottles were put aside, the dances ceased, the sirens wept aloud: the *Montagne*, flagship, had given the signal to weigh anchor. At once a long procession of sailors, soldiers and gunners took the road to the port and the boats which were waiting to take them aboard.

D AND E: AT TRAFALGAR, 1805

What follows are excerpts from the after-action report of the *Redoutable*'s Captain Lucas at Trafalgar. They show that the fighting at Trafalgar may not have been as entirely one-sided as is often thought:

I was at the head of my officers walking along the batteries: throughout I found the lads burning with impatience to begin the fight, several saying to me: 'Commander, don't forget to board them.' At 11.30 the enemy raised their colours. The *Redoutable*'s

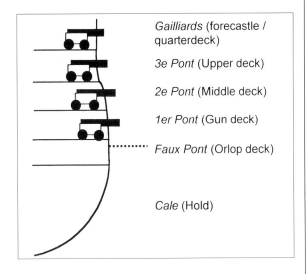

Gailliards (forecastle / quarterdeck)

3e Pont (Upper deck)

2e Pont (Middle deck)

1er Pont (Gun deck)

Faux Pont (Orlop deck)

Cale (Hold)

Diagram showing a cutaway view of a French three-decker. The guns on the *gaillards* actually meant that there were four levels of guns on these mighty ships. Battery height on the gun deck could be as low as 5½ft and its close proximity to the waterline meant the gun ports would have to remain closed in poor sea conditions. The 80- and 74-gun warships omitted a middle gun deck.

the yards. The *Victory*, unable to pass the French flagship to stern, came alongside us, in a manner that our poop deck found itself alongside and above its quarterdeck. From this position the grapnels were thrown across to them. Those at the rear were cut, but those ahead resisted, our broadsides were discharged at point blank. This resulted in a horrible carnage.

F AND G: AT TRAFALGAR, 1805

The *Redoutable* and *Victory* soon became locked in close combat with both Lucas and Nelson exposed to danger on their respective quarterdecks. Although some have questioned his claims, Robert Guillemard leaves us with an account of how Nelson's mortal wound may have been inflicted:

All our top-men had been killed, when two sailors and four soldiers (of whom I was one) were ordered to occupy their post in the tops. While we were going aloft, the balls and grape-shot showered around us, struck the masts and yards, knocked large splinters from them, and cut the rigging in pieces. One of my companions was wounded beside me, and fell from a height of thirty feet upon the deck, where he broke his neck … When the English top-men, who were only a few yards distant from us, saw us appear, they directed a sharp fire upon us, which we returned. A soldier of my company and a sailor were killed quite close to me; two others who were wounded were able to go below by the shrouds. Our opponents were, it seems, still worse handled than we, for I soon saw the English tops deserted, and none sent to supply the place of those who must have been

Contemporary French engraving of a boat approaching Valetta harbour in Malta in 1798. Note the sash worn round the waist of the sailor standing behind the sail.

killed or wounded by our balls. I then looked to the English vessel and our own. The smoke enveloped them, was dissipated for a moment, and returned thicker at each broadside. The two decks were covered with dead bodies, which they had not time to throw overboard. I perceived Captain Lucas motionless at his post, and several wounded officers still giving orders. To the rear of the English vessel was an officer covered with orders, and with only one arm. From what I had heard of Nelson, I had no doubt that it was he. He was surrounded by several officers, to whom he seemed to be giving orders. At the moment I first perceived him, several of his sailors were wounded beside him, by the fire of the *Redoutable*. As I had received no orders to go down, and saw myself forgotten in the tops, I thought it my duty to fire on the rear of the English vessel, which I saw quite exposed and close to me. I could even have taken aim at the men I saw, but I fired at hazard among the groups I saw of sailors and officers. All at once I saw great confusion on board the *Victory*, the men crowded round the officer whom I had taken for Nelson. He had just fallen, and was taken below, covered with a cloak.

The account of the battle is continued by Lucas, who claims to have come within an ace of capturing Nelson's flagship:

The decks were strewn with dead and wounded and Admiral Nelson was killed by our musket fire. Immediately the *Victory*'s decks were evacuated and the vessel ceased to fire. But it was difficult to cross over to it because of the movement of the ships and the height of its third deck. I ordered the main yard's cables to be cut so as to use it as a bridge. *Aspirant* Yon and four matelots got onboard by means of *Victory*'s anchor and told us there was no one in the

The 1813 inauguration of Cherbourg harbour, in presence of the Empress Marie Louise. The Revolutionary navy suffered from the lack of a major Channel port.

batteries. At the moment when our lads were about to follow them, the *Temeraire*, which had seen that *Victory* was no longer fighting and was inevitably about to be taken, came full sail ramming us to starboard. We were riddled at point-blank by the fire of its artillery. It is impossible to express the carnage produced by that murderous broadside. More than two hundred of our lads were killed or wounded, as was I at the same instant, but not badly enough for me to be prevented from remaining at my post.

Following the intervention of the *Temeraire*, the *Redoutable*'s fate was sealed. When finally its colours were struck only 169 of 643 crewmen remained alive, 70 of whom were wounded. The shattered remains of the ship were abandoned the following morning and the *Redoutable* was left to sink in bad weather.

H: MATELOT, 1804

Before the Revolution, sailors were not issued with uniforms by the navy but were expected to provide their own clothing or to have the necessary *hardes* (clothes – lit. rags) deducted from their pay. In consequence sailors were found in the traditional dress of their native regions, as seen in plates B and C. However, on 4 February 1794, the Republican government made a provision that each matelot or novice would receive a sack containing the following *hardes*: six shirts (two white, four blue), two pairs of overalls, a round hat, four pairs of stockings (including two woollen pairs), two pairs of shoes, a hammock and blanket, three jackets, three waistcoats, a bonnet and four handkerchiefs.

Also shown are: (1) Hammock shown both rolled and suspended for sleeping in with a blanket. (2) A wooden

gamelle and biscuits, with a *bidon* (3) which held the wine ration for a seven-man mess. (7) Shows a typical boarding grapnel, the larger variety of which would be hung from the yards and would fall down onto an enemy ship in the event of a collision, while the smaller ones (a *grapin à main*) could be thrown by hand. Boarding axes (5) fulfilled a number of functions: they could be used as weapons and to cut away grapnels or the ropes to enemy gun ports when two ships came alongside. The spikes at the back edge of the axe could be driven into the hull of an enemy ship, providing a foothold to allow sailors to clamber up higher vessels. Grenades (6) were most effective when dropped from the rigging onto crowded enemy decks below. They were lit by a match and had a fuse that burned for about six seconds. The cutlass (4) was perhaps the most famous of all boarding weapons with its crude guard and wide blade perfect for close-in fighting.

A *grand canot* (main boat) from a French ship of the line by Baugean.

INDEX